MESSAGE OF THE SACRAMENTS

Monika K. Hellwig, Editor

Volume 2

Gift of Community

Baptism and Confirmation

by

Thomas A. Marsh

A Michael Glazier Book
THE LITURGICAL PRESS
Collegeville, Minnesota

Typography by Peg McCormick and Dick Smith

  Printed in the United States of America.

2   3   4   5   6   7   8   9

Library of Congress Cataloging-in-Publication Data

Marsh, Thomas A.
    Gift of community : baptism and confirmation / Thomas A. Marsh.
        p.   cm.
    Reprint. Originally published: Wilmington, Del. : M. Glazier,
1984. (Message of the sacraments ; 2).
    Includes bibliographical references.
    ISBN 0-8146-5228-X (Liturgical Press)
    1. Baptism—Catholic Church.   2. Confirmation—Catholic Church.
3. Catholic Church—Doctrines.   4. Catholic Church—Liturgy.
5. Initiation rites—Religious aspects—Catholic Church.   I. Title.
II. Series: Message of the sacraments ; 2.
BX2205.M38   1990
234'.161—dc20
                                                        90-40963
                                                          CIP

For
Eorann

CONTENTS

EDITOR'S PREFACE

This volume is one of the series of eight on *The Message of the Sacraments*. These volumes discuss the ritual practices and understanding and the individual sacraments of the Roman Catholic community. Each of the eight authors has set out to cover five aspects of the sacrament (or, in the first and last volumes, of the theme or issue under discussion). These are: first of all, the existential or experiential meaning of the sacrament in the context of secular human experience; what is known of the historical development of the sacrament; a theological exposition of the meaning, function and effect of the sacrament in the context of present official Catholic doctrinal positions; some pastoral reflections; and a projection of possible future developments in the practice and catechesis of the sacrament.

There is evident need of such a series of volumes to combine the established teaching and firm foundation in sacramental theology with the new situation of the post-Vatican II Church. Because the need is universal, this series is the joint effort of an international team of English-speaking authors. We have not invited any participants whose writing would need to be translated. While we hope that our series will be useful particularly to priests, permanent deacons, seminarians, and those professionally involved in sacramental and catechetical ministries, we also address ourselves confidently to the educated Catholic laity and to those outside the Roman Catholic communion who are interested in learning more about its life and thought. We have all tried to write so as to be easily understood by readers with little or no specialized preparation. We have all tried to deal with the tradition imaginatively but within the acceptable bounds of Catholic orthodoxy, in the firm conviction that that is the way in which we can be most helpful to our readers.

The Church seems to be poised today at a critical juncture in its history. Vatican II reopened long-standing questions about collegiality and participation in the life of the Church, including its sacramental actions, its doctrinal formulations and its government. The Council fostered a new critical awareness and raised hopes which the Church as a vast and complicated institution cannot satisfy without much confusion, conflict and delay. This makes ours a particularly trying and often frustrating time for those most seriously interested in the life of the Church and most deeply committed to it. It seems vitally important for constructive and authentically creative community participation in the shaping of the Church's future life, that a fuller understanding of the sacraments be widely disseminated in the Catholic community. We hope that many readers will begin with the volumes in this series and let themselves be guided into further reading with the bibliographies we offer at the ends of the chapters. We hope to communicate to our readers the sober optimism with which we have undertaken the study and thereby to contribute both to renewal and to reconciliation.

Monika K. Hellwig

Chapter One

CHRISTIAN INITIATION: GENERAL CONCEPT AND CONTEXT

The sacraments of christian initiation are baptism, confirmation and the first eucharist. Only when one has received all these sacraments is one a full member of the Church, able to participate fully in all aspects of its life. These sacraments thus form a complex unity which is full christian initiation. They represent stages advancing to a climax which is full participation in the eucharist. Participation in the eucharist is the achievement of christian initiation. The eucharist is a celebration of full membership of the Church, the Body of Christ, for the eucharist is the Church in its most significant moment. These ceremonies thus constitute the way a person is initiated into the Church and becomes a full member of it, a full Christian, with all that that means and involves. Christian initiation is initiation into the christian community and its life.

The eucharist, as the climax and achievement of christian initiation and the central action of the Church's life and being, requires a study to itself and is so treated in this series on the sacraments.[1] Baptism and confirmation constitute

---

[1]Ralph A. Keifer, *Blessed and Broken: An Exploration of the Contemporary Experience of God in Eucharistic Celebration,* Message of the Sacraments 3, (Delaware: Glazier, 1982).

the sacramental introduction to the eucharist and thus form a unity in themselves. This work is devoted to a study of these sacraments and the unity which they form as sacraments of christian initiation.

This short and simple description of christian initiation immediately raises further and deeper questions and invites to further investigation. It will be the task of this study to attempt to undertake that investigation, to identify and illuminate these questions and issues. But meanwhile, in this introductory chapter, what is perhaps most needed is a general context, a horizon, an outline map, within which all consideration of these sacraments and the issues they involve may be situated. It is only too easy to presuppose and take for granted this context or horizon. We always tend to take for granted the familiar and the usual, often to the point of not really seeing them. The general context of christian initiation requires some examination and definition and this will be our first task. We can begin with the term initiation itself and the concept it represents.

Initiation signifies an introduction, a beginning, a beginning of participation in something. Christian initiation is such a beginning; it is a beginning of something fundamental and profound, something intimately connected with life itself so as to share something of life's meaning and mystery, of its pain and its joy. This analogy of natural life and christian life can be fruitfully pursued further, for it involves the further analogy of birth as initiation into life and baptism as initiation into christian life, an analogy which is totally independent of the accidental fact that the vast majority of the subjects of baptism happen to be new-born infants.

At birth we say a baby enters the world. This simple statement is worth examining by considering its seemingly simple terms: baby, world, entering. Babies are so familiar a part of our experience that, like all things familiar, we take them for granted. But in doing so, we blind ourselves to the mystery which a baby is. A baby at birth is an empty capacity to participate in the world and its life. It is utterly dependent on others for the development of this capacity.

But does a baby at birth really enter the world? Is world here not too vast, too grandiose a term? A baby is born to a father and mother and so enters an existing family which is situated in a particular place at a particular time. It is immediately localized. It is initiated into a *local* community and destined to imbibe and share its local culture. It is immediately a local, a native.

However, once we begin to reflect for a moment, this term "local" begins to expand. Thus, for example, a baby born in Maynooth in 1982 is also born in County Kildare, in Ireland, in Europe, and so in the world in the late twentieth century. In and through its very local community and culture, the baby is introduced into the world and its life at a particular time. So it is true to say that a baby at birth enters the world. A baby at birth is a citizen of the world.

One may describe this aspect as the horizonal dimension of birth — birth, as it were, reaching across the present-day world.

This consideration, however, only invites us to further and deeper reflection on the mystery which is birth. The newborn baby, as we have said, has the capacity to participate in the world and its life but is utterly dependent on others for the development of this capacity. In terms of seeing the world and understanding it, it is blind and requires others to open its eyes and give it vision. An understanding of life, the world, reality, a way of seeing and thereby of participating in these, has to be given to the infant and child, mediated to it. This understanding, this way of seeing life and reality, is given in terms of the local culture into which the baby is born. Reality is interpreted, expressed and so seen in its terms. It is this outlook on life and reality given to the child as it grows up within this community which will determine the way it takes hold of its existence and shapes it. A 1982 Maynooth baby, therefore, will get a Maynooth, County Kildare, Irish, European late twentieth century view of life and the world. It will look out upon and view life and the world from this position in space and time.

This horizontal dimension, however, with its particular

world-view, is not as it were suspended, unsupported in time and history, as if it suddenly just appeared today or yesterday and did not really form part of time and history. The view of the world and reality mediated to the child by its community is not something of today or yesterday; it has a past, a history; it is a *tradition*, in the living sense of that term, given expression in the culture of that community and indeed constituting its life. To be integrated into that community, to become a member of it, is to see with its eyes, to share its vision, to look out upon the world and life from its view-point. That view-point is a tradition mediated by history. To become a part of that community, therefore, is to participate not only in its present, but also in its past, its history. Birth as initiation into life thus has not only a horizontal dimension spreading outwards in the present but also a vertical dimension reaching back into the past and indeed forwards into the future.

An understanding of birth as initiation into life and the world thus involves an understanding of the present local community with its life and culture into which the baby is born, of the tradition which that community embodies and of the history which mediated and mediates that tradition. Birth as initiation into life is a place where the beams of a cross intersect, beams which represent the horizontal and vertical dimensions of the event: local community and world, tradition and history.

Like birth, christian initiation also is an initiation into life, life as seen and lived by a community, this particular christian community with its tradition mediated by its history. An understanding of christian initiation within this context requires consideration of its horizontal and vertical dimensions, of the local community as a particular expression of the wider and ultimately world-wide christian community, of the tradition and the history which has formed this local community. It is from these elements that one discovers the factors which disclose the basic nature of this community, which reveal the character and calibre of the members who form it, of the vision of life which they possess and from which they live. In this way one can come to understand what initiation into this community means.

Pursuing this approach, one looks first at what we have called the horizontal dimension, that is, at the existing community. It is a community which has a vision of life which is total, which embraces life in all its breadth and depth, in its alpha and its omega. This vision is the community's faith, its way of seeing life and reality, of taking hold of existence, its way of living.

This vision or faith is a tradition borne by history. It has been handed down, it goes back. The illumination of the present is possible only by illumination from the past. The community is explicit about this; it explicitly appeals to the past. It can only explain itself by reference to the past. If we follow this tradition back through its history, we go back ultimately to the original, foundational christian community, the Jerusalem community after Pentecost, the Apostolic Church of the New Testament, and behind these to the disciples of Jesus, to the nucleus of the Twelve, to Jesus of Nazareth himself and the events of his life. This is where the community has its origin and its explanation. The vision or faith which today forms and sustains it is a vision and faith deriving from Jesus of Nazareth, "the mind that was in Christ." It is clearly impossible here to sum up that mind in a few words. But one can summarily say that it was determined by Jesus' consciousness of God as his Abba-Father, his own sonship of God and his mission to share that vision with men so that by associating with him in discipleship they could share in his relationship with his Father in the power of the Spirit. To share this mind thus meant adopting a fundamental attitude towards life and reality that was all-determining. It meant the formation around Jesus of a community who opened themselves to it in life. That community becomes the vehicle of that vision or faith in history, a community bearing its tradition perpetuating itself in history.

In its passage through history, the community does not and cannot escape from the ambiguities of the human condition, from that Original Sin which has stained the human heart and being. It is not lifted out of human history but remains fully embedded in it. It therefore comes through history with wounds and battlescars, the marks of its sins and failings. For it ever remains in and part of the world, the world which groans in travail awaiting redemption. But because it has seen a great light and responded to that vision, it ever retains the courage to acknowledge its sins, to repent, and to renew its hope in the light which is its life. But neither has its history been all one of failings. The vitality and creative power of its faith and hope have always been in evidence and its achievements through the centuries make a rich and impressive heritage. This community, in its passage through history, absorbs and gathers to itself to become part of itself and expressions of itself all the riches which human genius has been able to offer it — in spirituality, theology, philosophy, art, literature. Today this community and it alone is heir to this impressive heritage. There is only one way to share this heritage and the vision it expresses; that way is to become a member of this community of the disciples of Christ, to be given and to receive his vision, mind and spirit, sharing his relationship with the Father, living from this vision and relationship and being borne by them into God who is man's future. If it means, as it does, having to bear the failings and negativities of christian history, it also means being able to call one's own the christian achievements of the centuries which have given expression in so many various ways to this vision, mind and meaning of Christ — the achievements of the Patristic Age, of the great Cappadocians, of Augustine; of the Middle Ages, of Aquinas and Francis of Assisi, of Gothic architecture and art; of the Renaissance, of Dante, Michelangelo; of modern times, Pascal, Descartes, Newman. A roll-call of history's greatest figures. One who enters the christian community is given this legacy as his or her own. Henceforth they are at home with them, for they belong and are part of their house, their community, their history, their identity.

Because christian initiation is initiation into the christian community, the Church of Christ, its meaning is the meaning of the Church in all its richness and complexity. This is its general context, its horizon, the contours of its map. The suggestion of a horizontal and vertical dimension, of the intersecting beams of a cross, provides, I hope, a way of focusing into a single vision this horizon in all its vastness. It directs our attention to local community and world in the present, to tradition and history in the past, and invites us to see these as the unity they are. Externally, christian initiation is a very local event which normally takes place at the font and altar of the local community. But we must not allow the simplicity of the event to hide from us its profound character. However humble that local church and its font may appear to be, it has the dignity and beauty of a bride, the Bride of Christ. It draws its life from deepest roots. Its tradition is a store-house of all the best which the children of her history are able to offer her. Her deepest identity is the mind of Christ living in her, Christ who in the Spirit unites her to himself and gives her access to the Father. All this she bestows on the one she initiates and that is why her initiation ceremonies are so rich in symbolism and expression. The expressiveness is an inherent necessity. The climax of her initiation process is the eucharist. Here she is most truly and fully herself, for the eucharist is a mirror of all that the Church is, of all that she should be. There in the breaking of bread she recognises Him who is her life.

Part I
Origin and Beginnings:
The Early Church

Developments which continue through history, unless they totally contradict and reverse themselves, remain stamped by the character given them in their origin. To understand them, therefore, the period of origin requires special consideration. Christian initiation is such a development. Both its outward form and inner meaning are determined in its origin and all later developments, whether of rite or insight, are in one way or another developments of this structure, flesh on these bones.

A study of christian initiation must therefore pay special attention to its origin in the early Church and attempt to discover the spirit and form of this process at its birth. This constitutes Part I of our study. Once this foundation is laid, we will be in a position to consider and situate and understand later developments in the practice and understanding of initiation in the history of the Church. This will be Part II of the study.

Chapter Two

APPROACHING THE SOURCES

St. Luke in describing the reaction of the audience to St. Peter's sermon on Pentecost morning states: "So those who received his word were baptized, and there were added that day about three thousand souls". (Acts 2:41). This simple statement records the earliest practice of christian initiation and already some of its basic features appear. For the moment we may mention one of these. The phrase "there were added" shows that there is question of adding individual persons to an already existing body of people, that group, in fact, who had received the gift of the Spirit that morning in the upper room and whose number, according to St. Luke with his fondness for round biblical figures, consisted of one hundred and twenty (Acts 1:15). This group constituted the original, foundation community of what would yet become known as the Church of Jesus Christ. As Acts 2:41 states, baptism was the ceremony whereby this community received new members. It was the rite of initiation of new members into the Church.

But if so much is clear from this text of Acts, many other things are not and remain as questions to be asked. Granting the basic historicity of the text — and the evidence suggests we should grant it — we are not told for example, why the community selected this rite as its initiation ceremony. Why did this rite suggest itself? What did the rite comprise and involve? What was its precise meaning? These and many other questions here suggest themselves and seek an answer. The New Testament, however, does not give any simple answers to these questions. Nowhere does it give us a systematic presentation of its understanding of baptism and christian initiation. Its direct references to baptism are not, in fact, that numerous and even where they do occur they are usually incidental to some other topic. The writers of the New Testament were obviously able to take baptism for granted as the familiar rite it was to their readers. They do not therefore envisage the kind of direct question we tend and wish to ask and so do not directly provide the kind of information we seek. This information has to be inferred from the incidental allusions to baptism in the New Testament. But since no one text or passage sums up all that the New Testament has to say on this subject, we have to use all the relevant texts to build up the data we need to answer our questions. It is only in the light of the whole presentation of christian initiation throughout the New Testament that we can answer these questions.

An example will illustrate the necessity of this procedure. Most people, if asked what was the origin of christian baptism, would surely reply that it was commanded and instituted by Jesus Christ himself. They would be able to point to two texts from the Gospels which appear to assert this direct link between the commanding word of Christ and the Church's practice of baptism.

> He said to them: "Go into all the world and preach the gospel to the whole creation. He who believes and is baptised will be saved; but he who does not believe will be condemned". (Mark 16:15-16).

> Jesus came and said to them: "All authority in heaven and on earth has been given to me. Go therefore and make disciples of all nations, baptizing them in the name of the Father and of the Son and of the Holy Spirit, teaching them to observe all that I have commanded you; and lo, I am with you always, to the close of the age".
> (Matthew 28:18-20)

In former times, when the Gospels were regarded as accurate reporting of the events they related, such an appeal would have been granted without dissent. These were actual words spoken by Christ who here formally instituted baptism as the sacramental rite of initiation into the Church.

Today, however, biblical scholarship will not allow such a simple appeal to the words of Christ in the Gospels and where these two texts are concerned a number of factors counsel caution. There is, first, the general character of the Gospel material which is seen today not as direct reporting of the events of Christ's life but as the early Church's confession of faith in him and understanding of his history. This view prohibits the simple assumption that a text of the Gospels has historical value; each text has to be examined on its own merits. Further, in these two texts we are faced with the words of the risen Christ. From the nature of the case the Gospel material dealing with the Resurrection and appearances of the Risen One has peculiar difficulties of its own and scholars are especially cautious in this area. Again, these texts are clearly what may be called insitutional texts — they explicitly present Christ as instituting the sacrament of baptism. Scholars are again cautious where such texts are concerned, because the Church's interest in establishing such a foundation for its practice is obvious and there is at least the possibility that it may have expressed its belief in Christ as the source of its life and institutions in what we would regard as too simplistic a manner. Finally, there is the explicit assertion of the doctrine of the Trinity in the Matthew text. All the rest of the evidence of the New Testament leaves no doubt that this explicit understanding and assertion of faith in the Trinity was a development in the early Church and that it was not and could not have been formulated in so explicit a manner prior to Pentecost.

For these and other reasons one cannot simply assume the historicity of these texts. Nowadays, therefore, they cannot provide, as formerly, the starting-point for a study of baptism and christian initiation in the New Testament and the early Church. One cannot now simply proceed from the direct command of Christ to the execution of that command in the practice of the early Church, thereby explaining the origin of christian baptism. Rather these texts must themselves be seen as part of the early church's presentation of baptism, as evidence of its understanding of its initiation practice. It is as such they must be approached and interpreted. Today, then, the study of christian initiation in the New Testament must begin with the early Church's practice and the meaning which this practice expresses as this is presented in the New Testament as a whole. It is only in the light of this presentation that one can now assess the relation between this practice and Jesus of Nazareth. In other words, the place of Jesus Christ in the origin of christian baptism and initiation must be derived from the early Church's practice and understanding of it; it is not available to us directly apart from the situation in the early Church recorded in the New Testament.

The procedure, then, for studying the question of the origin and meaning of christian initiation in the early Church is to examine the New Testament as a whole to discover what this initiation practice was and what meaning was attached to it. This procedure, however, is not as simple as it sounds and presents its own problems. The New Testament is not a simple, homogeneous body of literature. It was written by different writers with very different backgrounds and interests and at different periods over a span of perhaps three-quarters of a century, a period of time, moreover, which was one of intense activity in the growing Church and which saw rapid and often disconcerting development. The New Testament, as one would expect, reflects this evolving situation and this can sometimes make it difficult to focus properly the situation which a particular document describes and out of which it was written. Moreover, most of the New Testament documents come from a period and situation in this era when the basic development in early Christianity had already taken place. They therefore tend to see and present earlier moments, whether it be the ministry of Jesus or the early years of the Church's life, in terms of the developed position they have now attained. They tend to read back the later development into earlier situations. This in no way means that these documents are without historical value for these earlier periods. But this can be discerned only if they are approached carefully and methodically and provided their own literary character is understood and respected.

In the area which concerns us here, christian initiation, the focus required to place what the various documents have to say in a true perspective may be found by noticing two different types of statement in the New Testament references to baptism and christian initiation. One type simply describes *the event* of initiation, either the actual initiation of some person or the procedure this involves. These may be termed Narrative Texts. The other type is concerned with the *meaning* of christian initiation and its main purpose is doctrinal. These we may term Doctrinal Texts.[1]

The first type, Narrative Texts, is found mainly in Acts of the Apostles and indeed most of the information that the New Testament provides on the early Church's initiation practice comes from this document. These texts of Acts provide the obvious starting-point for a study of the early practice of christian initiation and thus also provide the true setting for a study of those doctrinal texts where we see the Church trying to develop and deepen its understanding of its practice. The doctrinal texts of major interest occur mainly in the writings of Paul. Though Luke wrote later than he, Paul is far more advanced theologically. This creates its own problem when one approaches a theme which spans the whole New Testament. Since the genuine Pauline letters are the earliest written documents of the New Testament, it is tempting to begin one's study with this material. But Paul's theology is so personal, so developed and advanced, especially in comparison with Luke's, that it is simply not representative of the Church generally in the first century. If one begins with this Pauline material and then, following a chronological order, moves on to the later

[1] I take this useful distinction from A. George, "A Literary Catalogue of New Testament Passages on Baptism," in A. George *et al., Baptism in the New Testament,* (London: Chapman, 1964) 13-22.

documents, it is often difficult to avoid the impression that the Church's understanding of a theme such as initiation contracted and narrowed rather than expanded and deepened. Luke, though later than Paul, is more representative of early Christian thought and gives us a better picture of the early situation in the Church. He thus enables us to focus and understand better the developments which occur, especially the theological thought of Paul and John which presupposes this earlier situation and general level of thought.

These historical and literary factors determine the method of approach to our topic which we will adopt. Our interest will centre first on the early practice of christian initiation in the Church. We will be concerned here with what the Church did and what it meant by what it did in this practice. Here our chief sources will be what we have called narrative texts. As these texts occur mainly in the Acts of the Apostles we will here be mainly concerned with this document, though we will find that some material from the Gospels, such as the texts of Mark and Matthew already mentioned, also belong in this context.

We will then consider the deepening understanding of this practice which now occurs in the Church. As we will not be able, in a study as limited as this, to take account of all New Testament passages bearing on initiation, we will confine ourselves to the thought of St. Paul, who was the originator of this deeper theology and ever remains its greatest representative.

But before we begin this study of christian initiation in the early Church, there is another question which must claim our attention. Like Christianity itself, the christian initiation practice was a historical development; it did not drop suddenly from heaven into history. It has a background in history, in Judaism and the history of Israel, which explains many of the elements which the early Christians adapted to form their initiation rite and provided the concepts which shaped their understanding of this practice. An understanding of the origins and meaning of christian initiation requires consideration of this background and this must be our starting-point.

Chapter Three:

BACKGROUND: WATER AND THE SPIRIT

"Those who received his word were baptized" (Acts 2:41). Luke is very casual in this reference to the first occurrence of christian baptism. Clearly he could presume his readers' familiarity with the practice. But the modern reader is liable to ask some questions here. What is this "baptism" that is here so casually mentioned as a feature of the life of the Church on this its very first day? How does it come to make this sudden appearance? Baptism did not form any part of the ministry of Jesus and yet it is presented here as an important practice of the Church from its very beginning. However original the christian practice in itself may have been, it can scarcely have been a totally new invention. It must have had some background in previous and contemporary history. It is this question of the background to christian initiation that we here propose to consider. Two themes dominate the presentation of christian initiation in the New Testament: water and the gift of the Spirit of God. Our consideration of background will consist in a study of these themes in the Old Testament and Judaism.

Water

TERMINOLOGY

The early christian vocabulary, which the New Testament records, provides an interesting starting-point for our study.[1] We find there both the verb "to baptize" and the noun "baptism". The original Greek, however, has really two verbs "to baptize" and two nouns for "baptism". The Greek terminology, in other words, has important subtleties which modern translations find it difficult to match. In ordinary Greek usage the basic verb here was "baptein" which meant simply "to dip in, under" and was the term used for "to dye". But Greek also had an intensive form "baptizein" which was a transitive verb meaning "to immerse (something, someone)" and had the sense of going under or perishing. These verbs were seldom used in the sense of "to wash" or "to bathe". When we turn to Jewish Greek we find the Septuagint, the Greek translation of the Hebrew Old Testament, using "baptein" to translate the Hebrew word "to dip" and reserving "baptizein" for the hebrew *tebilah,* the technical term for purificatory washings and religious or cultic baths.

Turning to the New Testament we find that "baptein" is used there only in its ordinary sense (cf. Luke 16:24; John 13:26; Apoc 9:13). "Baptizein" is here reserved for the religious context, either for purificatory washing (once, Mark 7:4) or, more usually, the religious or cultic bath. In the New Testament, therefore, this term has a technical religious meaning and reference and is the technical term for "to baptize". Here the New Testament reflects and continues Septuagint and Jewish Greek usage. But the New Testament use of nouns for baptism is especially significant. It has two nouns, *baptismos* and *baptisma,* which in meaning and reference are quite distinct. *Baptismos* is the term used of Jewish water rituals (Mark 7:4; Heb 6:2; 9:10), while *bap-*

---

[1] On the baptismal terminology of the New Testament, see A. Oepke, *Theological Dictionary of the New Testament,* (Grand Rapids: Eerdmans, 1964+), I, 529-546.

tisma, a new word not found outside these christian documents, is the technical term reserved for the christian rite. Oepke's comment on this distinctive usage is to the point: "Since the New Testament either coins or reserves for christian baptism (and its precursor) a word which is not used elsewhere and has no cultic connections, and since it always uses it in the singular and never substitutes the term employed elsewhere, we can see that, in spite of all apparent or relative analysis, it understands the christian action to be something new and unique".[2]

This rapid glance over early christian baptismal terminology reveals that the background to christian baptism is Jewish, not Greek. The meaning of the Greek terms used in this context in the New Testament is determined by their Jewish usage, not by their meaning in ordinary Greek. The christian terms thus have a Jewish background while at the same time they break free from the background and take on a new and unique meaning. Christian baptismal terminology acknowledges and points out its own background in the ritual use of water in Judaism.

WATER AND RITUAL

There is a passage in the Gospel of Mark which reveals the place and prominence of this ritual in Judaism at the time of Christ.

> The Pharisees, and all the Jews, do not eat unless they wash their hands, observing the tradition of the elders; and when they come from the market place, they do not eat unless they purify themselves; and there are many other traditions which they observe, the washing of cups and pots and vessels of bronze.
>
> (Mark 7:3-5)

It is clear from this passage that for the Jews of Christ's time water had a deep ritual and religious significance. This was the seed-bed from which the christian practice of baptism was taken. How did Judaism come to see and use water in this way? The answer to that question lies in the ideas, practices and regulations of the Old Testament.

For the people of Israel, as for all ancient peoples, signs and symbols had great importance because it was in and through these that they expressed and lived their view of life and the world. Such symbolic expression was based on and consisted in the adaptation of some natural phenomenon. The Israelites were a land people to whom the sea was always strange and hostile. But precisely because they were a people of the dry land, they were only too conscious of the necessity of water, above all rainfall, to render this dry land fertile. Their existence depended on this irrigation and so water was both a real condition and a symbol of life for them. It was also from its natural use a symbol of cleansing and purification. On this natural foundation of water as a means of life and cleansing, the Old Testament built a system of symbolic actions where water was the symbol expressive of the reality intended. This is the Old Testament system of lustral or purificatory rites codified in the Mosaic Law and put in writing especially in the Book of Leviticus.

The basic concept behind these lustral rites was a very physical concept of impurity. There was no question here of a moral impurity contracted through deliberate personal sin. This concept of physical impurity derives from primitive animistic ideas and taboos which pervaded the religious thinking of ancient times. Israel, being part of its cultural and historical environment, inherited these ideas and practices, though it also elevated and purified them in a way consistent with its own monotheistic faith. We can gain some idea of the outlook which underlay the purificatory system by noting some of the main notions which formed that outlook.[3]

Man as such was regarded as unworthy to approach the all-holy, majestic deity; to do so represented an act of *lesé-majesté* and would mean his annihilation. To approach the

[3]See G. R. Beasley-Murray, *Baptism in the New Testament*, (London: MacMillan, 1962), 1-10.

deity, therefore, man had to be rendered worthy through a
rite of purification. (Cf. Exod 19:10-14; 29:4; 2 Sam 12:20;
Lev 16:4; Judith 12:7).

In its view of man the Hebrew world differed from the
later thought of Greek philosophy which saw man in terms
of two separate components, body and soul. The Hebrew
concept belonged to an older, more primitive outlook and
it had a unitary view of human nature and the human person. Man was here regarded as one being, a body-soul unit.
Hence, defilement of the body meant simply the defilement
of the person, of man. As this defilement was contracted
physically through the body, so also it could be removed
physically through the body undergoing a purification rite.

The multiplicity of ways in which the body, and so the
person, could contract uncleanness requiring purification
was determined by the concept of demonic powers active in
the world, particularly in circumstances connected with
birth, sickness, death. A person involved in these circumstances, for example, through touching a corpse, tomb,
certain animals, was regarded as defiled by this contact and
hence as requiring purification. Out of this background the
Mosaic Law elaborated a whole system of purification rites
whereby the defilement contracted in these various ways
could be removed. Among the rites so used lustral or washing rites were the most prominent. The natural power of
water for cleansing underlay this symbolic religious use, but
present also was the ancient idea of divine power operating
in running water that is, rivers and streams, where such rites
often took place. In a broad sense of the term we already
find here a sacramental use of water: such rites expressed
and effected purification from contracted defilement and
rendered the person worthy to enter God's presence and
worship Him. This purpose is significant for the future
christian context because it involves a ritual bath as a means
which prepares a person to enter the presence of God for
worship. (Cf. Exod 19:10-13; 29:4; Lev 16:1-4; 2 Sam 12:20;
Judith 12:6-9).

These Old Testament purificatory rites provide the basis
for a significant development when the great prophets of

Israel find in them an appropriate imagery to portray the meaning of the future messianic salvation. On the one hand, the plight of Israel harassed by her enemies and apparently abandoned by Yahweh is presented as land rendered infertile and desert through lack of water. Correspondingly, the future saving act of God is depicted as a watering of this dry land and a cleansing of its people. Chapter 35 of Isaiah, a hymn of thanksgiving which "hails the final victory of Yahweh, conceived of as having already taken place," is one of the best examples of this prophetic motif and imagery:

> The wilderness and the dry land shall be glad, the desert shall rejoice and blossom; like the crocus it shall blossom abundantly, and rejoice with joy and singing. ...Say to those who are fearful of heart: 'Be strong, fear not! Behold, your God will come with vengeance, with the recompense of God. He will come and save you.' ....For waters shall break forth in the wilderness, and streams in the desert; the burning sand shall become a pool, and the thirsty ground springs of water.
>
> (Isaiah 35:1-7)

Renewal of land and people go together in this prophetic perspective of the messianic salvation but the renewed land is also an image of the renewed people and this brings to mind the purificatory ritual of water as an image of the saving act of God. Isaiah 44:3-4 states: "For I will pour water on the thirsty land, and streams on the dry ground; I will pour my Spirit upon your descendents, and my blessing on your offspring. They shall spring up like grass amid waters, like willows by flowing streams".

The most significant of these passages in the prophets is Ezechiel 36:24-28:

> [24]For I will take you from the nations, and gather you from all the countries, and bring you into your own land. [25]I will sprinkle clean water upon you, and you shall be clean from all your uncleannesses, and from all your idols I will cleanse you. [26]A new heart I will give you, and a new spirit I will put within you; and I will take out of your

flesh the heart of stone and give you a heart of flesh. [27]And I will put my Spirit within you, and cause you to walk in my statutes and be careful to observe my ordinances. [28]You shall dwell in the land which I gave to your fathers; and you shall be my people, and I will be your God.

Commenting on this passage J. Muilenberg writes:

> 25. Yahweh will sprinkle clean water upon them to purify them from the stain and guilt of the past. 26. But the transformation goes deeper. He will give them a new heart, a disposition and will responsive to his purposes and requirements. .... 27. He will do yet more: his gift of a new spirit will enable them to render him the obedience which is his due. 28. In the renewed land they will renew the covenant bond. Blessings will abound.[4]

In these descriptions of the messianic renewal and salvation the imagery of the prophets associates together the purificatory ritual of the Mosaic Law and the eschatological saving act of God. God's saving act is here presented as a divine purificatory rite, a purificatory bath. But this act, it should be noted, is only a first step, and a negative step at that. It is preparatory and preliminary to the positive stages of the renewal just as purificatory rites were preparatory and preliminary to entering God's presence for worship. The passage in Ezechiel is the fullest and most explicit of these descriptions. As Muilenburg notes, each verse here marks a new stage in the renewal. Thus, the first stage, v. 25, represents the preparatory act of purification aimed at removing "the stain and guilt of the past" (Muilenberg *in loco*). This purification is a negative condition for the positive effects which follow. These consist of the moral and religious renewal of the people, v. 26, and God's final gift, the gift of his Spirit, v. 27. The significance of this passage

[4]J. Miulenberg, *Peake's Commentary on the Bible*, M. Black, H. H. Rowley, eds., (London: Nelson, 1962), 586.

for an understanding of christian initiation in the early Church will concern us again. For the moment, our concern is simply to note the elevated symbolic significance given to the purification rite by the prophets when they use this image to depict the purificatory aspects of God's saving messianic act.

Meanwhile, the reference in this passage of Ezechiel to the gift of the Spirit already introduces us to the second of the biblical themes which form the background to christian initiation, the theme of the Spirit of Yahweh.

The Spirit of God

The theme of the Spirit of God runs throughout the whole Old Testament and is too extensive a topic to be treated here in any depth. We will concentrate on the salient points of the concept which are relevant to an understanding of christian initiation and form an important element of its essential background.[5]

The term "spirit", in Hebrew *ruah* and in Greek *pneuma,* originally meant a movement of air and hence came to be the word for wind and breath. To ancient man wind and breath were phenomena of mystery and religious awe, manifestations of divine presence and power. The breath of man indicated life, the supreme though precarious gift of God. The wind, one of the great mysterious forces of nature, was a manifestation of divine power, the "breath" of God active in his creation, a numinous reality. For the Hebrew people *ruah,* though the term could have many meanings, could be used to refer to an extraordinary exercise of divine power, an act of God. This concept, as other related concepts such as the word of God, the hand of God, allowed Hebrew thought to conceive of God's immanent action in the world and history while his being remained transcendent, in the high heavens.

---

[5]W. Eichrodt, *Theology of the Old Testament* (London: SCM, 1967), I, 46-68; G. T. Montague, *The Holy Spirit: Growth of a Biblical Tradition,* (New York: Paulist Press, 1976).

The period when the concept of the Spirit of God came to prominence in Jewish thought would seem to have been the time of the conquest and early settlement in the land of Canaan. Israel at this period relied on what one could call charismatic figures, persons who attained prominence and leadership through the extraordinary gifts which they displayed. Such were the leaders known as judges, the warriors such as Gideon and Samson, and the early ecstatic prophets. The significance and achievements of these persons were attributed to the Spirit of God coming upon them and acting in them. The figure of the prophet is especially significant here. The early prophets were ecstatic figures whose ecstatic frenzy was seen as possession by the Spirit and whose message was accordingly accepted as divine revelation through the Spirit. Because of Israel's great dependence on divine guidance and because at this period there was no structure in the community which could guarantee such guidance — no settled body of tradition, no permanent institution, no "scripture" in any canonical sense — the figure of the prophet was regarded as providing this guidance and the Spirit of God was seen as the source of his revelations. The inspiration of the prophet was the work of the Spirit and his message therefore was the word of God. This is the source of the Spirit's special association with divine revelation and prophecy. In the Old Testament the Spirit of God is above all the Spirit of prophecy (cf. Osee 9:7).

The Old Testament has also, however, another concept of the Spirit, which, though less prominent, is significant for the future. Hebrew thought, as we have said, had recourse to the concept of the Spirit to explain God's action in history. For the Bible God's first historical act was his act of creation and so we find in the biblical references to creation that the Spirit of God is presented as God's agent in this work. This is the concept of the life-giving Spirit, the Spirit of God as the source of created life (Gen 1:2; 2:7; Ps 33:6; Job 26:13; 33:4; Judith 16:14). However, since the original act of creation was a once-for-all event and did not require repeating, this life-giving function of the Spirit likewise has a once-for-all character and is not repeated. The concept of the *life-giving* Spirit is not a feature of the life of Israel and it is only referred to in the Old Testament where there is a reference back to the original creation. The great prophets, however, will find a new and significant role for this concept when they come to describe the Spirit's role in the messianic age.

Granted the role of the Spirit in God's guidance of his people through their history, it is not surprising to find that this theme has a significant place in the prophets' portrayal of the messianic age. The Messiah himself is here presented as endowed with a special gift of the Spirit for his work whereby he sums up in himself all the qualities of the great figures of Israel's history. This again is the classical concept of the Spirit of prophecy. For the Messiah will bring the final revelation, the final word and disclosure of God's saving purpose. (Cf. Isaiah 11:1-6; 42:1-4; 61:1-3). The prophets also speak of a gift of the Spirit for the whole messianic people, fulfilling the wish of Moses in Numbers 11, 29: "Would that all the Lord's people were prophets, that the Lord would put his Spirit upon them". This is what is envisaged in the famous prophecy of Joel 2:28-29:

> And it shall come to pass afterward, that I will pour out my Spirit on all flesh; your sons and your daughters shall prophesy, your old men shall dream dreams, and your young men shall see visions. Even upon the menservants and maidservants in those days. I will pour out my Spirit.

We have already seen that the prophets present the new age as involving a renewal of land and people. This idea naturally enough recalled the account of creation and led to the presentation of the messianic age as a new creation. The Spirit of God will again be the source of this new life; the Spirit will here again play a life-giving role. (Cf. Isaiah 32, 15-19; 44:3-4; Ezechiel 36:26-27; 37:10-15). This concept is expressed simply and directly, in words which clearly have Genesis 2:7 in mind, in Ezechiel 37:14, the passage which describes the vision of the dry bones: "I will put my Spirit within you and you shall live."

In the perspective of the prophets, therefore, the coming

new age will be marked by a new and universal gift of the
Spirit of God. This will be a gift of the Spirit of prophecy
bringing the final revelation; a gift of the life-giving Spirit
bringing into being the renewal of the new creation; it will be
the eschatological gift of the Spirit because it will remain
forever as God's final, permanent gift.

The two themes of water as ritual purification and of the
Spirit of God are thus brought together in the prophets'
presentation of the messianic age. They are related, constit-
utive elements of God's saving act ushering in the new age
and people. Ezechiel 36, 24-26 is the clearest and most
significant of these passages in the prophetic literature. God
will purify the people from their sins; then He will bring
about within them a true moral, religious renewal, a renewal
of heart; finally, he will place his Spirit within them to
ensure the effectiveness and permanence of this renewal.
The Spirit is here presented as the principle and source of
this interior renewal. The classic concept of the prophetic
Spirit which we find in the other prophets here expands to
embrace the concept of the life-giving Spirit as the agent of
this new creation. This daring prophecy will have great
significance for the development of the understanding of
christian initiation in the early Church.

The cleansing ritual of water is associated with only the
first of these states of renewal, the purificatory stage. But
water and Spirit are here closely associated in the one
context. A further, though accidental association appears in
the verb "to pour out" which now is often used for the gift of
the Spirit — cf. Isaiah 44:3; Ezechiel 39:29; Joel 2:28-29;
Zechariah 12:10. This verb could have a wide figurative
sense in Hebrew, as in most languages. One spoke of pouring out one's heart — Proverbs 1:23 (the Hebrew for "heart"
here is *ruah*). So also the gift of the Spirit came to be
described as God "pouring out" his Spirit. But this verb does
reinforce the already existing association of water and the
Spirit in the presentation of the messianic age.

Judaism

The prophets used concepts and practices of the faith of Israel to portray the saving act of God in the messianic age. We must now see how the Jewish people in the period after the exile, the period normally referred to by the term Judaism, responded to these ideas. Our interest will centre especially on the period of late Judaism, the period immediately before and contemporary with Jesus of Nazareth and early Christianity. We are concerned here therefore with the immediate background to christian initiation in the New Testament.[6]

In the centuries following the Exile the Jews developed a more rigid system of religious practices in an effort to assert and maintain their identity as God's people. The notion of purity and impurity was more strongly emphasized and the causes of uncleanness, and thereby the occasions requiring purification, were multiplied (cf. Mark 7:1-5). This period also saw a growing sense of the coming of the Messianic Kingdom and a corresponding urgency about being prepared for this coming. The prophets' relation in image of ritual purification and the eschatological act of God now in these circumstances began to take on a practical expression. In the period after 100 B.C. what is called a baptist movement spread throughout the region of Palestine and Syria. This was a practice of frequent ritual baths by various more or less unorthodox Jewish sects which were now springing into existence and whose basic concern was preparation for the Day of the Lord. The meaning of these baths was purificatory but the existence of this baptist movement reveals a heightened sense of rite in Judaism which associates the purificatory rite of baptism with the coming of the Kingdom of God.

Today the best known of these groups is the sect of the Essenes, knowledge of whose practice has been greatly

---

[6]See: J. Delorme, "The Practice of Baptism in Judaism at the Beginning of the Christian Era" in *Baptism in the New Testament*, A. George *et al.*, 25-62; G. R. Beasley-Murray, *op. cit.*, 11-30.

increased by the discovery of the Dead Sea Scrolls at Qumran. The Qumran community practiced a daily ritual bath as an important feature of their religious life. While this practice was basically concerned with ritual purification, it was much more closely related with interior dispositions and ethical behaviour than was the case with the Old Testament practices or the contemporary Jewish water purifications. Baptism here is seen as a sign and expression of interior dispositions and is moving towards a strong sacramental meaning. Man is spoken of in the Scrolls as the centre of a struggle between two opposed dispositions called the spirit of wickedness and the spirit of truth and the bath is concerned with promoting the victory of the latter.

Another form of baptismal practice that is a significant element in the immediate background to christian initiation is Jewish proselyte baptism. This was already in existence as a Jewish initiation rite for Gentile converts at the time of Christ.[7] The traditional rite of initiation into the people of Israel for males had always been circumcision. But at least by the first century of the christian era converts to Judaism, both male and female, had also to undergo a ritual bath or baptism which for males followed on circumcision and in the case of females was the only initiation rite. The meaning of this rite was once again purificatory. At this period the Gentile as such was regarded as impure. On entering Israel he or she had to be cleansed from this impurity to be fit to participate in Jewish religious life and worship. The baptism of the proselyte removed this impurity and immediately following it the new convert performed an act of sacrifice, thereby celebrating and proclaiming his or her full status as a member of the people of Israel. The significance of this practice as background to the emergence of christian initiation is obvious: the rite of baptism already exists here as an official Jewish initiation rite and it constitutes the immediate introduction of the convert into Jewish liturgy and worship.

[7]On this question, see: W. F. Flemington, *The New Doctrine on Baptism*, (London, 1948), 3-16; G. R. Beasley-Murray, *op. cit.*, 18-31, J. Delorme, *loc. cit.*

But the baptismal practice most closely related to Jesus of Nazareth and of greatest significance for the initiation practice of the early Church was that of John the Baptist.[8] According to the information given in the New Testament and other sources, John saw his mission as one of preparing people for the imminent coming of the Messiah and his Kingdom. The background of this thought is obviously the teaching of the prophets on the Day of the Lord and the judgment and purification this will involve. To escape this judgment and receive this purification a person must prepare himself through repentance and conversion. This was John's basic message: repentance and conversion in preparation for the coming Messianic Kingdom. His was essentially a prophetic mission, "to make ready for the Lord a people prepared". (Luke 1:17). To accomplish this programme John used the ritual of baptism in the Jordan. In this he displays relationship with the general baptist movement of the time and particularly perhaps with the Essenes, though there are also significant differences. The baptismal action of John was the visible way those who had heard his preaching expressed their assent to it and acceptance of it. In undergoing the rite they confessed their sins, expressed repentance and committed themselves to an ethically better life, all with a view to entering the Kingdom. Their baptism was a visible expression of their practical acceptance of John's preaching.

The ministry of John was much more closely ordained to the concept of the arrival of the Kingdom than any previous baptismal practice. It had a sense of immediate urgency about it, of being on the eve of the event. John contrasted his own baptism, a baptism in water as he said, with the baptism which the arrival of the Kingdom would itself involve, a baptism "in holy spirit and fire" (Matt 3:11; Lk 3:16). In this phrase John is using the term "baptism" figuratively to describe the act of God. "Spirit" and "fire" do not here refer to distinct elements of that act but rather different aspects of it. "Fire" refers to the purification aspects, the purification

---

[8]On the baptism of John, see: W. F.. Flemington, *op. cit.*, 16-24; G. R. Beasley-Murray, *op. cit.*, 31-44; J. Delorme, *loc. cit.*

of sinners and, probably, the judgment and con
of unrepentant sinners; "holy spirit" refers to the
blessings which the inauguration of the Kingdom bestows.
The "holy spirit" John speaks of here is the Spirit of God
and here again the background to his thought is the
prophets' description of the Messianic Age and the role
which they assign to the Spirit in that event.

The preaching of John the Baptist again brings together
the two threads we have been following in this discussion of
the background to christian initiation, water and the Spirit.
In turning our attention now to the concept of the Spirit in
late Judaism it must be stated clearly and explicitly — for
the question is often treated with great vagueness — that
this concept was the classic biblical concept of the Spirit of
prophecy. The prophetic revival of the notion of the life-
giving Spirit has simply not remained alive. In fact, by this
period an opposed notion dominates Jewish thought, the
concept of the quenched Spirit. Judaism came to believe
that following the last canonical prophets, Zecharia, Haggai
and Malachi, prophecy had ceased in Israel because God
had withdrawn the Spirit of prophecy on account of the sins
of the people. The Spirit of prophecy was quenched and
would return again only with the appearance of the Messiah
and the inauguration of the messianic age. Then, as the
prophets had foretold, God would fulfill Moses' wish and
endow the whole community of faithful Israel with his gift
of the prophetic Spirit, the crowning gift of all the messianic
blessings. When, therefore, the Spirit of prophecy returned,
this would be a sign that the final age had dawned.

Meanwhile, in Hellenistic Judaism and unorthodox
Palestinian groups such as the Essenes, a somewhat different approach was beginning to emerge.[9] This concept of the
Spirit derives from the prophetic tradition and basically
belongs to it, but it is characterised by a more humanist
approach which relates very closely the notions of the Spirit
of God and the human spirit. This is the concept of the Spirit
of prophecy influenced by the Wisdom tradition. This tradition prized a right interior spiritual disposition and it saw

[9]See J. Delorme, *art. cit.*, 32-48.

this disposition as produced by a true understanding of God's will and law. Knowledge and understanding moulded personal character and determined human behaviour. Hence the central importance in this outlook of Wisdom, a true understanding of God and his ways. Such Wisdom was a gift of God, indeed it was God himself communicating himself to the human mind as enlightenment. It is easy to see how this outlook could absorb the prophetic concept of the Spirit. The Spirit of God is here identified with Wisdom and is presented as the source of spiritual understanding and consequent right behaviour in man (Wis 7:7, 27). While this outlook thus tends towards a somewhat humanist notion of the Spirit, it also remains faithful to the prophetic tradition of Israel in looking forward to the final messianic gift of the Spirit who will bring the ultimate revelation of God, Wisdom in the definitive sense, and will be God's crowning gift to man. John the Baptist's reference to "baptism in holy spirit and fire" should probably be seen as influenced by this outlook.

At the time of Christ, therefore, Judaism as a whole looked forward to the gift of God's Spirit which the inauguration of the Messianic Kingdom would involve. In one way or another, the prevailing concept of this gift was that of the Spirit of prophecy who would bring the final revelation of God and his will for man and who would be God's eschatological and crowning gift to man.

Already by the time of Christ the biblical themes of water and Spirit had come to image and portray the great saving act of God in the inauguration of the Messianic Kingdom. John the Baptist is able to sum it up in a phrase: "baptism in holy spirit and fire". Despite the many variations of these themes, the dominant description of this act in biblical literature remains the passage in Ezechiel 36:24-26 with its three stages: purification; interior moral and spiritual renewal; the gift of the Spirit. The first two of these correspond to the negative and positive sides of the conversion which the new age will involve. The third is God's final and crowning gift, the eschatological gift which expresses and guarantees the permanence and finality of the new age.

Chapter Four

FOUNDATION AND PRACTICE

Jesus, Baptism and the Spirit

While the Old Testament and Judaism provide the background to christian initiation, they do not constitute its foundation. That belongs to the person and history of Jesus of Nazareth. Christian initiation represents the reaching out to men of the redemption which Jesus accomplishes and which he himself is. A full discussion on this topic would require a study in christology. As this cannot be undertaken here, it must remain presupposed. For present purposes, it must suffice to state that the disciples of Jesus, from their experience of him and the events of his history—the ministry, death, resurrection, outpouring of the Spirit—came to recognise him as the long-awaited Messiah, the Christ of God, through whom was inaugurated the Messianic Age with its blessings of forgiveness of sins, the gift of the Spirit and hope of resurrection.

These blessings were now the possession of this community of Christ's disciples who lived in the light of the Lord's presence and in the favour with God which his presence ensured. True, he was now glorified with God, "seated at God's right hand" (Acts 2:33; 7:55-56; Rom 8:34) and they awaited his *parousia* or Second Coming when the final consummation would take place. Nevertheless, the decisive

43

event had already occurred in the victory of Jesus which his resurrection constituted and disclosed and which the gift of the Spirit brought within their experience. The messianic blessings were now available in and through this community of faithful disciples and it was their missionary task to announce this gospel to all peoples and to offer all the opportunity to share in these blessings by becoming part of this community, fellow-disciples with themselves of Jesus the Christ. Christian initiation was the process whereby entry into this community was accomplished.

There is one question concerning the ministry of Jesus which for our purposes does merit some consideration here. We need to ask what contribution the ministry of Jesus may have made to the practice and understanding of christian initiation in the early Church. The first comment on this question must be a negative one: the practice of baptism did not form any significant part of the ministry of Jesus. Jesus himself, according to John 4:2, did not baptize.[1] Nor was the Spirit given in the course of the ministry. This was a post-resurrection event, a direct result of the exaltation and glorification of Jesus: "as yet the Spirit had not been given, because Jesus was not yet glorified" (John 7:39). The later practice of christian initiation, therefore, has no actual antecedents in the ministry of Jesus. Nor could such outward antecedents, if they had existed, have possessed the same meaning as the later christian practice, since the realities, the messianic blessings, which this practice expresses and mediates, were still only in process of realization.

Yet, while all this is true, there remains the certain and significant fact that Jesus himself did receive the baptism of John in the Jordan and, according to the assertion of all the Gospels, that the Spirit of God descended upon him: "Jesus came from Nazareth of Galilee and was baptized by John in the Jordan. And when he came up out of the water, immediately he saw the heavens opened and the Spirit descending

---

[1]On the possible historical significance of John 3:22; 4, 1-2, see: W. F. Flemington, *op. cit.*, 30-31; G. R. Beasley-Murray, *op. cit.*, 32-67.

upon him like a dove" (Mark 1:9-10; cf. Matt 3:13-17; Lk 3:21-22; Jn 1:32). The early Church was quite definite that this event marked the beginning of the ministry of Jesus (cf. Acts 1:32; 10:37; the Gospels *in loco*). They saw it not just as a moment of mere time but as a moment of inner significance, as if John's baptism was somehow the logical and significant moment for the beginning of the ministry. The reason for this rests on the christian view that John was the immediate precursor of the Messiah and heralded his appearance. The whole expectant history of Israel was summed up in this lone figure who, pointing to Jesus of Nazareth, declared: "Behold, the Lamb of God, who takes away the sin of the world" (John 1:29). Jesus' baptism by John marked his acknowledgement of the validity of John's mission, of his call for repentance and conversion in preparation for the coming of the Kingdom. Jesus' submission to John's baptism and the fact that this event marked the opening of his own ministry gave John's baptism a special significance for Jesus and his followers.[2]

According to John himself his baptism pointed forward to and prefigured the eschatological baptism in holy Spirit and fire which would inaugurate the Messianic Age and constitute its people. The themes of baptism and the Spirit recall and indeed are directly dependent upon the images used by the prophets, the images of cleansing purification, of renewal of heart, of the outpouring of the Spirit. In the baptism of Jesus these images are focused together in his person, on the eve, as it were, of the fulfilment of these prophecies. When the decisive events of Jesus' death and resurrection and the outpouring of the Spirit had occurred, the disciples of Jesus recognised that prophetic image had here attained actual fulfilment. What had been symbols projecting the future could now therefore act as symbols expressing the decisive event. The event of Christ represented in historical fact the culmination and fulfilment of the history of Israel, the dawning of the Messianic Age. In

[2]See: G. R. Beasley-Murray, *op. cit.*, 45-66; R. E. O. White, *The Biblical Doctrine of Initiation*, (London: Hodder and Stoughton, 1960), 90-109.

the hope of Israel the image of baptism and the outpouring of the Spirit had come to sum up and express this event. The prophetic symbols had now issued in reality. This reality had continued existence as the possession of the community of Jesus' disciples, constituting its very being. The admission of new members to the community constituted an act of self-expression by the community. It had here to give expression to its being. The prophetic history of Israel, the experience of Judaism and the baptism of Jesus provided the symbols for this expression, the symbols of baptism and the giving of the Spirit.

The Early Church

Understanding presupposes experience since it is an understanding of experience. Christian initiation was an established practice in the early Church before its deeper meaning and implications were thought out and stated. St. Paul was the first to wrestle with this deeper meaning of christian initiation but by this time this process was already an established practice for over two decades. Paul is trying to develop a deeper insight into something which is already established. A study of christian initiation in the early Church must therefore begin with an examination of this practice before attempting to follow Paul's analysis of its meaning. The practice itself incorporates its own meaning and is an expression of a concept, an understanding. It is a statement in action. Our task in examining this practice is to study this statement, to identify this meaning.

We are fortunate to possess in the Acts of the Apostles a document which takes us behind the thought of Paul to the practice which he presupposes and analyses. Acts is not a formal theological treatise, as the Pauline letters are in many ways, but a narrative recounting the life of the Church in its early years and especially the story of its missionary expansion. It thereby enables us to see, in some measure at least, the early Church's way of life, its way of thinking and acting, in a way a theological treatise could never do. On the question of christian initiation there are a number of passages in Acts which *narrate* the occurrence of this event, or some element of it. These passages are descriptive rather than theological but the narrative implies a theological meaning and reveals to us the basic original significance of the Church's rite of initiation. All subsequent theological speculation on this rite will be an effort to penetrate more profoundly this original and basic understanding.

These texts of the Acts of the Apostles will form the basis of our study of the early rite of christian initiation. We shall see that the so-called institutional tests of Mark 16:15-16 and Matthew 28:18-20 also belong in this context. However, as we will not be able to discuss all the relevant texts of Acts individually, we will concentrate on one particular passage, Acts 2:37-41. Though this passage is somewhat summary in form, it is nevertheless the fullest and most interesting of these statements and when corroborated or, where needs be, filled out from the other sources, provides the most comprehensive statement on christian initiation in this whole document. It will thus enable us to effectively telescope and focus a large issue without getting involved in a detailed exegesis beyond the scope of this study. Our interest will not be confined to particular aspects or features of christian initiation as presented in these texts, but will embrace also *the context in the life of the Church* to which initiation belongs and in which it occurs and *the coherent structure* which the rite possesses. These texts reveal this context and structure and it will be an important part of our task to identify them.

This passage forms the conclusion to Luke's account of Peter's sermon to the wondering crowd on Pentecost morning. Peter declares here that the history of Israel has found its promised fulfilment in the resurrection and exaltation of Jesus of Nazareth and the outpouring of the Holy Spirit: "Now raised to the heights by God's right hand, he has received from the Father the Holy Spirit who was promised, and what you see and hear is the outpouring of that Spirit" (v, 33). In other words, the messianic age has dawned and the outpouring of the Holy Spirit is a sign of this event and the availability of the messianic blessings which it involves.

Peter then concludes his sermon with the christological statement which is its culmination: "For this reason the whole House of Israel can be certain that God has made this Jesus whom you crucified both Lord and Christ" (v. 36).

The narrative now turns to the crowd's reaction to Peter's announcement and in doing so introduces its reference to the first occurrence of christian initiation in the history of the Church. The audience inquire: "What must we do" (v. 37). Peter replies as follows:

> You must repent and everyone of you must be baptized in the name of Jesus Christ for the forgiveness of your sins; and you will receive the gift of the Holy Spirit (v. 38).

The final outcome is then reported:

> They were convinced by his arguments and they accepted what he said and were baptized. That very day about three thousand were added to their number (v. 41).

This whole sermon (Acts 2:14-36) introduces us to an early form of the preaching of the Gospel, an example of the primitive kerygma. The context in question here is thus the typical missionary context: the Gospel is preached; its message is a demanding one; acceptance of it requires one to abandon one's former vision and way of life, acknowledge one's failings and commit oneself to the new vision and way of life of the gospel of Christ. Christian initiation finds its place as the conclusion and culmination of this missionary enterprise. This is historically its first context and it is its logical context. Christian initiation is concerned with conversion to christian faith as a result of hearing the christian gospel.

Having thus identified the basic context of initiation, we can turn our attention to the elements which make up this event and the structure which they form. The repentance and conversion which the acceptance of the gospel demands consists in a turning away from the past and a commitment to a new way of life in the future. Acceptance of the gospel implies this personal decision for conversion. But in itself this purely personal decision is not sufficient to appropriate what the message promises. This decision must lead one forward to "baptism in the name of Jesus Christ", if the forgiveness of sins and the gift of the Spirit are to be received. The private decision for faith and conversion is in itself incomplete and defective until the further steps of baptism and reception of the Spirit have been taken.

BAPTISM

The baptismal action referred to here is a ritual bath in water similar to that of the Jewish proselyte rite or the baptism of John. The distinctive character of the christian rite is indicated by the formula "in the name of Jesus Christ". This formula expresses the meaning and significance of the christian rite and distinguishes it from all other outwardly similar ritual baths. The formula occurs frequently in the baptismal contexts of Acts (2:38; 8:16; 10:48; 19:5; 22:16) and similar expressions elsewhere in the New Testament show that the formula had a technical status in the early Church. (Cf. 1 Cor 1:13; 6:11). The meaning of the phrase should therefore throw some important light on how the early Church understood its rite of baptism.

The expression "in the name of" was an idiom in both Greek and Aramaic in the first century and it had a basically similar meaning in both languages, though there was a difference in the context of its usage.[3] In Greek it was a commercial or banking expression, equivalent to our own "to the credit of", "to the account of". It expressed ownership, the name on the account. In Aramaic the phrase was used to express the status of a personal relationship or the purpose or result of an action establishing such a relationship. A significant analogy in Judaism to its use in the early christian baptismal contexts was the practice whereby a heathen slave entering the service of a Jewish household received a baptism "in the name of slavery", that is, with a view to becoming a slave of the master of the house. The

[3]A. Oepke, TDNT, I, 529-30; G. R. Beasley-Murray, *op. cit.*, 100ff.

formula expressed the meaning and purpose of the action
and the relationship of belonging and service which it established. Baptism "in the name of Jesus Christ", then, would
mean entering into the service of Christ and into personal
relationship with him as one's lord and master, becoming
his follower. It meant assuming and bearing the name of
Christ, becoming a Christian. The act of baptism was the act
which formally effected and established this relationship.
The initial personal decision for faith and conversion logically culminated in this act and its promise and potentiality
are realized in this act.

Our passage goes on to further describe this baptism "in
the name of Jesus Christ" as being "for the forgiveness of
your sins". Clearly it is stating here the effect of the rite.
Forgiveness of sins means, broadly but basically, the remov-
al of the barrier which separates man from God and therefore the reconciliation of man with God or the salvation of
man. This is the messianic blessing *par excellence,* the very
meaning of the Kingdom of God and the salvation it
involves. This is the messianic purification and renewal of
which the prophets had spoken and to which the whole
history of Israel had looked forward. In realizing personal
relationship and commitment to Christ, baptism gives participation in the salvation he has achieved. This salvation is
described here in the negative manner familiar to Judaism,
forgiveness of sins. Judaism was not able to provide early
Christianity with concepts that would do justice to the
positive aspect of this reality, union with God through
Christ.[4] Christianity will have to develop such concepts
itself, an enterprise in which St. Paul will play a particularly
significant role.

THE GIFT OF THE SPIRIT

Having spoken of baptism "in the name of Jesus Christ
for the forgiveness of sins", Peter now mentions a new

[4]See S. Lyonnet in S. Lyonnet and L. Sabourin, *Sin, Redemption and Sacrifice:
A Biblical and Patristic Study* (Rome: Biblical Institute Press, 1970), 32-33.

element in the process of christian initiation: "and you will receive the Holy Spirit". A whole number of questions arise here with regard to this reference. What concept of the Spirit of God is in question? Why is the Spirit mentioned here in this first occurrence of christian initiation? Does receiving the Spirit go with the forgiveness of sins and thus represent an aspect of the effect of baptism? Is there any question of an external rite associated with this giving of the Spirit, in the way the act of baptism is associated here with the forgiveness of sins?

The bare reference in the text to receiving the Spirit would not seem to offer much hope of finding an answer to all these questions. We have to remember, however, that this text does not stand alone; it has a background in the Old Testament and Judaism which we have touched upon already, and it is connected with other references to the giving of the Spirit in Acts which may also help us. With the aid of these sources we may be able to throw more light on these questions than might at first sight appear.

The first question we have to consider is why the Spirit is mentioned here at all. It is obvious from the whole narrative of this second chapter of Acts that the Spirit which Peter promises his audience is the gift which he and the other disciples received that Pentecost morning. It is the Spirit of Pentecost which is in question here, the Spirit which descending on the disciples had made them into a community, the community of the Spirit-filled disciples of Christ. The Spirit is mentioned, therefore, because Peter is here inviting his audience to become part of that community and this means receiving or sharing in the Spirit which now fills it. But there is also another reason. We have seen that the gift of the Spirit of God figures prominently in the prophets' description of the messianic age. The outpouring of God's Spirit would be the sign of that age's arrival and the crowning gift of its messianic blessings. Peter's whole sermon is an announcement that the messianic age has now arrived in Jesus Christ and that the experience of Pentecost is the promised gift of the Spirit. The conclusion of his sermon is an invitation to his listeners to believe this message and receive the blessings that are now available, forgiveness of sins and the gift of the Spirit. There is therefore no mystery to the reference to the Spirit in this context.

But what concept of the Spirit of God is implied here? How is the Spirit understood? The answer to this question is again ready to hand in the text of Peter's sermon. Peter presents the outpouring of the Spirit at Pentecost as the fulfillment of the prophecy of Joel. This is the Spirit of prophecy, the Spirit which enables God's message to be forcefully preached and accompanies the preaching with powerful signs. These also are the effects of the Spirit given at Pentecost, as this very sermon of Peter bears witness. We must remember too that this was the persisting concept of the Spirit in contemporary Judaism. It is therefore the only concept of the Spirit one can conceive in the minds of Peter and his audience. It is the prophetic Spirit that is envisaged in this text.

The other questions we have mentioned — whether the gift of the Spirit is, with forgiveness, an effect of baptism or occurs after baptism, and whether there is question of an external rite — these questions are all inter-connected. It is the issue whether Acts of the Apostles sees the gift of the Spirit as an effect of baptism or as a post-baptismal gift. It must first be said that the text in question here, v. 38, does not clearly state that this gift *is* an effect of baptism. This is often too easily assumed in commentaries. Rather, the use of the future tense — "and you will receive the gift of the Spirit" — and especially the change of grammatical mood from imperative ("be baptized") to future indicative strongly suggest that a temporal sequence is envisaged here, that is, that the Spirit is received after baptism.[5]

Other considerations confirm that this is the correct interpretation. The Spirit understood as the prophetic Spirit is not related in the Old Testament or in Judaism with the type of purification which forgiveness of sins involves. It is a distinct concept which describes the power of God acting in

[5]See N. Adler, *Taufe und Handauflegung* (Münster, 1950), 27.

men irrespective of their moral status. It would be strange, therefore, if these concepts were so related here in a passage which we are justified in regarding as describing the thought and practice of the Church in its very early days. And since the passage clearly presents forgiveness as the effect of baptism, baptism also is here involved in this distinction. The presentation of christian initiation throughout the Acts of the Apostles shows that this view is the correct one. Throughout this document baptism and forgiveness of sins are consistently related together, whereas the gift of the Spirit is just as consistently presented as distinct and separate from baptism.[6] Indeed, in those key passages where Luke describes the *full* process of christian initiation, Acts 8:12-17; 19:1-7, the gift of the Spirit is an effect of a post-baptismal rite, imposition of the hands. We are therefore justified in viewing the gift of the Spirit referred to in this text as an event envisaged as occurring after baptism. In the process of christian initiation presented in this whole passage of Peter's sermon, the Spirit is a post-baptismal gift.

We now come to our final question: is there question of an external rite associated with this giving of the Spirit? Acts 2:38 states simply: "and you will receive the Holy Spirit". This is clearly a summary statement which in itself is open to different interpretations. It should be clear by now, however, that St. Luke in this whole passage presupposes a particular ceremony or rite of christian initiation. It is because he assumes the reader's familiarity with this rite that he feels entitled to summarise. This means that if we find elsewhere in Acts a more specific description of this rite, this will provide the correct interpretation of this summary statement. Now, as we have seen, there are two later passages in Acts where St. Luke describes the full process of christian initiation as he knows it, 8:12-17 and 19:1-7. In both of these cases the gift of the Holy Spirit is presented as the effect of the post-baptismal rite of imposition of hands. These passages are paradigmatic for Luke's understanding

---

[6]The following texts are significant: 5:31; 8:14-20; 10:43-48; 13, 24, 38-39; 19:1-6.

of the rite of initiation and this is the rite which must be presupposed in the context of his other summary references, unless there is clear evidence to the contrary. This applies to Acts 2:38: the summary statement "and you will receive the Holy Spirit" presupposes the initiation rite which is fully described in chapter 8 and 19 and therefore imposition of hands is also presupposed here as the external rite mediating the gift of the Spirit. That this is the correct interpretation is further confirmed by the fact that it coheres with the consistent presentation of baptism and the gift of the Spirit throughout Acts.

THE GIFT OF COMMUNITY

St. Luke does not neglect to inform us of the result of Peter's preaching on that first Pentecost. Following his account of Peter's invitation to his audience to accept christian initiation, he proceeds:

> Those who received his word were baptized,
> and there were added that day about three thousand
>   souls.
> They devoted themselves
> to the teaching of the apostles
> and to the fellowship (koinonia),
> to the breaking of bread
> and to the prayers.
>
> (Acts 2:41-42).

These statements give us the sequence of events which resulted from Peter's sermon for those who responded positively to his preaching. Their acceptance of the gospel he announced led to their actual baptism. This was the logical implication and conclusion to their decision for faith. "Baptism" here should not be understood as necessarily restricted to the rite of immersion, thereby excluding any suggestion of a further rite for the giving of the Spirit. This would mean reading too much into the occurrence of this term here. Nomenclature, except in very simple cases, often involves a rather simplistic telescoping of diverse elements.

"Motorcar" may be a simple word but it refers to a very complex and intricate object whose complexity and intricacy are little conveyed by the word itself. Christianity had to develop a new vocabulary to meet its needs. The natural preference for concrete rather than abstract terms was operative in this development. The term "baptism" thus came to be used, or could be used, as a shorthand for christian initiation. This is the most likely meaning of the term in this text.

The text states that those who were baptized "were added", that is, they joined the existing group of the disciples of Jesus as fellow-disciples with them. Their initiation meant initiation into the existing community, becoming members of that community. The following verse, v. 42, spells out what this involved. It gives a summary, a cameo, of the distinctive communal existence of the early christian community in which the new converts now fully participate. The activities described here are the distinctive activities of this community, the activities which mark them off from all others and define them. Joachim Jeremias has argued, cogently it seems to me, that we have here a description of the sequence of an early christian service: teaching; table-fellowship (the *agapē* meal): celebration of the eucharist; concluding prayers.[7] In any case, these are the elements which constitute the distinctive communal existence of the early Church in Jerusalem after Pentecost. The term "fellowship" (*koinonia*) became a common term in the New Testament, and especially in St. Paul, to describe membership of the Church and participation in its life.[8] Christian initiation means becoming a disciple of Christ in the fellowship of the community of his disciples. The celebration of the eucharist is the central and most distinctive exercise of this fellowship and discipleship. As initiation into the christian community and its life, christian initiation is a preparation for and introduction to the

---

[7] J. Jeremias, *The Eucharistic Words of Jesus* (London: SCM, 1966) 118-121.
[8] 1 *Cor* 1:9; 10:16; 2 *Cor* 8:4; *Phil* 1:5; 2:1; 3:10; 1 *John* 1:3.

community's central act of worship, the celebration of the eucharist.

In giving us this cameo of the Church's distinctive life in the context of his account of the first occurrence of christian initiation, St. Luke emphasises the community and ecclesial dimension of christian initiation. Christian initiation means becoming a member of the christian community and a full participant in its life. It means being given and receiving a new identity, a new name, a new life. It is the gift of community in Christ.

CONTEXT AND STRUCTURE

The summary statement of Acts 2:37-41, filled out with information gleaned from other references, enables us to identify and describe the context and structure of christian initiation in the early Church. The Acts of the Apostles presents a coherent picture here which cannot in any way be the effect of the author's editorial artistry but must be the inherent context and structure of the event itself. This structure of christian initiation may be outlined as follows:

1. The preaching of the gospel.
2. Acceptance of the gospel by the hearer, involving his or her personal decision for faith, repentance, conversion.
3. Baptism, where this decision is accepted by the community and the drive inherent in it attains its goal through relationship with Christ and the forgiveness of sins which that relationship involves.
4. Imposition of the hands for the giving of the Spirit.
5. Membership of the christian community and participation in its life.

This structure shows that the context to which christian initiation belongs in the early Church is the kerygmatic or missionary situation, the preaching of the gospel and the conversion which it is hoped this preaching will achieve. Initiation into the community is the goal of preaching the gospel. This context and structure can be discerned in all references to baptism and christian initiation in the Acts of the Apostles. This is the setting of christian initiation in the early Church and it is from within this setting that its true meaning and significance can be discerned.

THE INSTITUTION TEXTS

The identification of the context and structure of christian initiation in the early Church enables us now to situate and understand the so-called "institution" texts, Mark 16:15-16 and Matthew 28:19-20. We find here the same context and structure, the same pattern, as in the Acts of the Apostles. The text in Mark states:

> He said to them: "Go into all the world and preach the gospel to the whole creation. He who believes and is baptized will be saved: but he who does not believe will be condemned".

This text of Mark is quite laconic in its statement. The more elaborate text of Matthew is of greater interest and significance.

> Jesus came and said to them:
> "All authority in heaven and on earth has been given to me. Go therefore and make disciples of all nations, baptizing them in the name of the Father and of the Son and of the Holy Spirit, teaching them to observe all that I have commanded you; and lo, I am with you always, to the close of the age".

The context once again is explicitly missionary. The passage opens with a statement of Christ's authority, his *exousia* as established in his resurrection and exaltation. This is the source and power of the christian mission. The missionary mandate of the Church, the community of his disciples, follows from this. They are commanded: "Go and make disciples of all nations". The first task is to preach the gospel, but the goal of this preaching is to make converts, "to make disciples". The term "disciple" here is of particular significance. The term does not occur in the New Testament outside the Gospels and Acts. Its primary meaning is as a designation for the body of Jesus' followers during his ministry, but, as its use in this text and in several passages of Acts shows, it was also used later as a description of members of the Church, Christians as they came to be called (Acts 11:26). This extension of the term from its original meaning as a term for the immediate followers of Jesus to embrace later converts and members of the christian community is important and significant.

In Acts 1:22, when describing those eligible to take the place of Judas as a member of the Twelve, Peter presents what may be regarded as a basic definition of the original meaning of the term: "one of the men who have accompanied us during all the time that the Lord Jesus went in and out among us, beginning from the baptism of John until the day when he was taken up from us . . . . . ". In this sense of the term there can be no extension of its application after the resurrection; the number it applies to is fixed. Yet the term was extended to later christian converts and members of the Church. These, too, in becoming members of the Church became disciples of Christ, Christians. The original disciples had met Jesus of Nazareth in the flesh, and heard his message of the Kingdom with its call to acceptance and commitment, had responded to this call and followed him. The later converts are also disciples of Jesus because they, too, have encountered him, not indeed in the flesh, but as the risen Christ present in his community — "I am with you always". In the preaching of this community the voice of Jesus, his message and his call, is still heard. To fully accept this kerygma of the Church means to answer this call of Jesus, it means becoming a member of this community where Christ is a living presence and where relationship with him can be established and lived. Conversion to christian faith means to become a disciple of the living Christ in the fellowship of his disciples. Baptism is the formal act whereby one seals and accomplishes this conversion, whereby one *now* becomes a disciple of Christ. Baptism is the climax of the Church's preaching mission because baptism is the formal act which accomplishes conversion and achieves discipleship. For these later converts baptism represents and replaces the meeting with Jesus in the flesh and the response to his call which was the origin of discipleship in the earthly ministry. The presentation in the Gospels of this meeting with Jesus and the life of discipleship which followed from it become primary sources for an understanding of the meaning of baptism.

These texts of Mark and Matthew thus present the same context, structure and significance of christian initiation as we found in the Acts of the Apostles. Baptism is the goal and climax of the Church's preaching and missionary endeavour. It means conversion to christian faith, becoming a member of the christian community, becoming a disciple of Jesus Christ.

FAITH AND BAPTISM

Some further information on the practice of baptism in the early Church which our documents provide now begin to fall into place. From the language and expressions used in Acts we can see that in the early Church to become a believer and to be baptized meant the same thing. An unbaptized believer is a being who has neither meaning nor existence for the early Church. Two texts from Acts must suffice here to illustrate this point. Acts 18:8, reporting the conversion of Crispus and other Corinthians, states: "Crispus, the ruler of the synagogue, believed in the Lord together with all his household; and many of the Corinthians hearing Paul believed and were baptized". Also Acts 19:2, where Paul asks the twelve he meets at Ephesus: "Did you receive the Holy Spirit when you believed?" In the Greek the verb "believed" in these texts has the aorist or past definite form. This tense form signifies a completed action at some definite moment in the past. This grammatical significance and the way the verb is used in these and other similar passages show that this moment is the moment of baptism. For the early Church to become a believer and to be baptized mean the same thing. Reception of baptism is the formal confession of christian faith. Christian faith is not a purely private act, a purely personal stance; it is a formal public act accomplished in the act of baptism where one becomes a member of the Church, a Christian, a believer.[9]

This equation of the first profession of faith and baptism suggests that a formal confession of faith was involved in the reception of baptism. We find some positive indications that this was so in the texts of Acts. Thus, in Acts 22:16, Ananias is reported as saying to Paul at Damascus: "Rise and be baptized and wash away your sins, calling on his name". This "calling on the name" of Christ most likely means a christological confession of faith in Jesus.

The preaching of the Church was directed towards this confession as its climax and conclusion. Peter's Pentecost sermon, for example, concludes: "Let all the House of Israel know assuredly that God has made him both Lord and Christ, this Jesus whom you crucified" (Acts 2:36). Acceptance of the christian kerygma involved some such confession and if the act of baptism represents the formal moment of faith such a confession at this moment is only to be expected. We know from the Pauline letters that the expression "Jesus is Lord" was a standard summary and confession of faith in Christ (e.g. Rom 10:9; 1 Cor 12:3; Phil 2:11). The source of this christological confession and of its popularity may very well have been the early baptismal liturgy.

Further confirmation of this suggestion may be seen in the account of the baptism of the Ethiopian eunuch reported in Acts 8:36-38, where the Western text has a verse, v. 37, which states: "And Philip said: 'If you believe with all your heart you may (be baptized)'. And he replied: 'I believe that Jesus Christ is the Son of God'." (The actual baptism then follows). Though this text is generally, and no doubt rightly, regarded as interpolated, it is nevertheless very early, certainly not later than the early second century, and must be accepted as reflecting much earlier baptismal practice. It thus provides corroborating evidence that baptism in the early Church involved a public confession of faith.[10] In its

[9]O. Cullman, *Baptism in the New Testament* (London: SCM, 1950), 54: "Baptism is the starting point of faith."

[10]J.N.D. Kelly, *Early Christian Creeds* (London: Longmans, Green, 1960²) 40-42.

early and original form this confession was probably purely
christological, such as those just mentioned, "Jesus is
Lord", "Jesus Christ is the Son of God". The heavenly voice
at the baptism of Jesus in the Jordan acknowledging him as
Son of God (Mark 1:11; Matt 3:17) may also be connected
with this practice and further evidence of it. This would
certainly be true, if, as I believe to be the case, the whole
scene of Jesus' baptism as presented in the Gospels is meant
to be a type of christian baptism and thereby reflects its
actual form.

It is now clear from our documents that baptism as
understood in the early Church had a primarily christological reference and significance. It signified relationship and
commitment to Christ, discipleship. This purely christological reference, however, could not remain isolated in itself
but had to lead on to consideration of the relationships
which were significant for Jesus, especially that with the
God he called Abba, Father, and the role of the Spirit of
God in his life as the Church came to understand this. The
reference to baptism in the text of Matthew shows us the
Church's growing awareness of this implication. Baptism
here is no longer said to be "in the name of Jesus Christ" but
"in the name of the Father and of the Son and of the Holy
Spirit". Relationship with Christ is now recognised to
involve relationship with the Father and the Spirit. The
christological reference of baptism has here expanded to
acknowledge explicitly the trinitarian dimension which was
always implicit in it. That Matthew's text does not stand
alone as evidence for this development is clear from the
similar text in the early christian document The Didaché
which at this point is probably contemporaneous with Matthew or very nearly so, and from the evidence of the later
baptismal liturgy, even as early as the Apostolic Tradition
of Hippolytus (c. 215). The trinitarian confession of Matthew, in other words, is evidence of the early development of
the trinitarian baptismal creed.[11]

[11]J. N. D. Kelly, *ibid*.

Finally, this association of faith and baptism alerts us to the different actors in the ceremony of baptism and their different roles. Baptism here exhibits both an objective and a subjective aspect. Objectively, it is an act of the community, the Church, who invites and performs, and, at a deeper level, of the living Christ and God his Father. The act of the Church is a sacrament, a realizing expression, of the act of Christ and in him of the Father. Subjectively, baptism is an act of the recipient who responds to the Church's invitation to accept and believe its gospel, makes its faith his own in his confession of faith and allows himself to be appropriated by Christ as his disciple in the fellowship of his community of disciples. Both these dimensions are essential to the meaning of baptism.

A COMMAND OF JESUS

We can now consider the question whether Jesus gave an actual command to his disciples to baptize. Does an authentic saying of Jesus underlie the texts of Mark 16:15-16 and Matthew 28:19-20? Is this the origin of christian baptism? There can be little doubt that these texts have been influenced and shaped by the later practice of the Church. They reflect this practice and its context too clearly not to be in some form a product of them. Moreover, both texts as they stand have to be considered for various reasons late formulations. The Matthew text has the trinitarian formula which cannot be a primitive feature, while the Mark text belongs to that section at the end of this Gospel, 16:9-20, which biblical scholars are convinced is an addition subsequently added to the original text.

All these considerations, however, do not exclude the possibility that these texts may go back to a simpler form of statement made by Jesus to his disciples which was then later adapted to suit the actual conditions of the Church. Arguments can be adduced in support of this position. If Jesus commanded the disciples at the Last Supper with reference to the eucharist: "Do this in remembrance of me" (Lk 22, 1 Cor 11:24-25), one could argue for the likelihood of a similar command to initiate new converts by baptism. One could argue that the existence of baptism from the very beginning of the Church as its initiation rite can only be explained by a direct command from Jesus himself. On the other hand, it is difficult to be certain about the issue and in fact the question is not as important as is often supposed. The mission to preach the gospel and make disciples, and therefore to adopt an initiation rite such as baptism, is already inherent in the disciples' experience of the risen Christ. The event of the Resurrection is already mission and mandate. The event itself is already a statement awaiting verbal expression; the mission texts simply put it into words. The command to baptize may be such an expression.[12]

But whichever position one adopts regarding these texts, the christian mission to preach the gospel, to make converts and initiate them into fellowship, does come from Jesus himself, from the mission of his life and the victory he achieved. In this sense the practice of baptism is founded on a command of Jesus to his Church.

Conclusion

In what I have been describing as narrative texts, especially from the Acts of the Apostles and the Gospels, the early Church has given us a clear and coherent picture of its practice and understanding of christian initiation. The context of initiation in the life of the Church is the missionary situation, the preaching of the gospel. The aim of this preaching is to convince the listeners that Jesus of Nazareth is the Christ, the Son of God, and that salvation is available in his name, that is, through discipleship of him. Converts join the existing community of Christ's disciples and participate in its life.

Christian initiation is the process whereby they enter and become members of this community. This process consists,

[12]See G. R. Beasley-Murray, *op. cit.*, 77-92.

apart from the necessary preparatory instruction, of two rites, baptism "in the name of Jesus Christ" for the forgiveness of sins and imposition of hands for the giving of the Spirit. These effects represent the messianic blessings, the salvation which the victory of Christ has realized and made available and which is now the possession of the community of his followers. It is the mission of this community to announce this salvation to all men and invite all to enter into fellowship with them.

The reason why christian initiation in the early Church consisted of two rites seems puzzling to us, but this is mainly because we attempt to read back into this early period the situation and understanding of later times. But if we reflect on the Old Testament and Jewish background of Christianity, the seed-bed from which it sprang and from which, at least in the beginning, it drew its concepts, language and practices, and if we relect also on the disciples' experience of Jesus and the events of his history, this practice becomes much easier to understand and in fact appears quite logical. Ezechiel, summing up the messianic prophetic tradition, had described the blessings of the new era as involving three stages: cleansing purification, renewal of heart, the crowning and sealing gift of the Spirit of God. The place of ritual lustration in Judaism, the prevalence of the ritual bath and the whole contemporary baptist movement, giving the ritual bath an initiatory character, all this made baptism an obvious initiation rite for the early Church, especially in view of John's practice and Jesus' own baptism by him.

Imposition of hands was also a traditional Jewish rite and it could have different purposes and meanings. It was used, for example, at the ordination of Levites, where it was a community gesture and signified that the community here poured its personality, its character, into these chosen men who could henceforth therefore act as their representatives and substitutes. This is the concept we find in Acts 8 and 19: Peter, John and Paul in imposing hands on the newly baptized act in the name of the Spirit-filled community and by this gesture they extend this Spirit-character of the community to these recipients.[13] The personality of the community as the Spirit-filled community of the disciples of Christ is shared with the baptized who thereby receive the Spirit. The rite is here an initiation gesture which expresses a particular aspect of becoming a member of this community, namely, sharing in its Spirit-filled character. The Jewish background of Christianity thus provided the elements of concepts and rites which the early Church was able to adapt and fuse together to form its own process of initiation with its own special significance.

But the immediate origin of christian initiation, as we have seen, that which gave it its special meaning and significance, was the person and history of Jesus of Nazareth, his ministry, death, resurrection, the out-pouring of the Spirit. Here also we find the immediate reason for the practice of two rites in christian initiation. Baptism, as we have seen from the early Church's practice and understanding, has a christological significance. It is concerned with discipleship and enables one to join the original community of Jesus' disciples, those whom he himself had gathered and who had remained faithful to him. It was because of and subsequent to their experience of Jesus that these disciples experienced the outpouring of the Spirit — "as yet the Spirit had not been given, because Jesus was not yet glorified". (John 7:39).

These two events, the event of Christ and the event of the Spirit, were distinct events in their historical experience. But these were the two events which made them the community they now were. Prior to Pentecost (Acts 1), they existed as the community of the disciples of Jesus; following Pentecost (Acts 2), they were the *Spirit-filled* community of the disciples of Jesus. When they now came to receive new members into the community, to associate others with themselves, they repeated in sacrament, in effective symbol, the two founding salvation events which brought them as a com-

[13]See D. Daube, *The New Testament and Rabbinic Judaism* (London, 1956), 224-246.

munity into existence and which expressed and explained the nature and character of this community: baptism representing the event of Christ, hence the christological emphasis; imposition of hands representing the out-pouring of the Spirit, the pneumatological aspect.

Later christian thought will see the unity of these events which originally were experienced separately. But this will be an achievement of theological insight. The early practice of christian initiation is not constructed from a worked-out, developed theology; it is founded on the salvation events as they have been historically experienced. Seen in the light of this whole background and this immediate history, the two rites of christian initiation appear logical and coherent.

It is important to note however, that the practice of initiation in the early Church is not quite adequate to the vision of the new age described by Ezechiel. He had spoken of three aspects: cleansing purification — renewal of heart— the gift of the Spirit. In its beginning the Church's understanding of its two initiatory rites was not able to fully embrace the prophet's thought. Baptism is here seen in somewhat too negative a way, "Forgiveness of sins." This certainly corresponds to the purification aspect in Ezechiel but it does not fully express the positive aspect of renewal of heart. Judaism did not provide early Christianity with a positive concept of this reality and christian thought had here a programme to develop. But from the beginning the Church did emphasize relationship with and discipleship of Christ as the central significance of baptism. A deepening understanding of what this means and involves will eventually lead to this positive concept, the messianic renewal of heart seen as life in Christ.

Finally, the concept of christian initiation in the early Church may be described as the gift of identity and community in Christ in the power of the Spirit. This concept of christian existence can be strongly sensed in a later passage of the New Testament, the opening verses of the First Letter of John. These verses capture and summarise the context and significance of christian initiation which the texts we have been studying contain and express.

That which was from the beginning,
which we have heard,
which we have seen with our eyes,
which we have looked on and touched with our hands,
concerning the Word of life—
the life was made manifest,
and we saw it, and testify to it,
and proclaim to you the eternal life
which was with the Father
and was made manifest to us—
that which we have seen and heard
we proclaim also to you,
so that you may have fellowship with us;
and our fellowship is with the Father and his Son,
   Jesus Christ.

                               1 John 1:1-3.

Chapter Five

DEEPENING UNDERSTANDING: BAPTISMAL THEOLOGY OF ST. PAUL

The understanding of christian initiation in the early Church, which the Acts of the Apostles preserves for us, could not remain unaffected by the profound development in christian thought which accompanied the Church's missionary expansion. The fulfillment of the history of Israel in Jesus Christ had at the same time transcended that history and its categories of thought. Almost from the beginning, the conceptual system and language which the first Christians took over from Judaism and pressed into service to express their new faith proved inadequate to this task. Of necessity, the search for a deeper understanding and a more adequate form of expression got under way. This effort eventually issued in the great theologies of the New Testament, especially those of St. Paul and St. John. As regards baptism and christian initiation, the fruit of this development is found above all in the writings of Paul. "Paul", writes Rudolf Schnackenburg, "is the first to give real impetus to the development of the theology of baptism in the primitive Church."[1] Paul's theology of baptism is without

[1]R. Schnackenburg in J. Bauer, ed., *Encyclopedia of Biblical Theology* (London: Sheed and Ward, 1976), 58.

doubt the high-water mark of early christian thought on this sacrament. Eventually, this Pauline theology will have a profound influence on the Church's understanding of baptism. It is the most profound and comprehensive statement of the meaning of baptism in the New Testament. There is every justification, therefore, for devoting this chapter exclusively to the thought of Paul.[2]

THE CONTEXT

There are several passages in the letters of Paul which contain a reference to baptism. Yet nowhere does he provide what could be called a formal treatment of the sacrament. These references, which are usually quite brief, are always incidental to some other topic which is his main concern. Further, Paul gives us very little information about the actual practice of baptism and christian initiation. He is not what we would call today liturgically minded. As far as the actual rites and practices of initiation are concerned, he was able to presuppose familiarity with these on the part of his audience. It was never his concern to describe them in his writings. This does not mean he regarded the rite as unimportant. This is certainly not true. But his main interest and preoccupation when mentioning baptism is the meaning of the sacrament and its continuing significance in and for the life of the Christian. His interest is entirely doctrinal and practical. His understanding of baptism is an integral part of his whole theological system and therefore involves this whole system.

Paul shows in many places his familiarity with the general context and structure of christian initiation as practiced in the primitive Church. His frequent use of aorist verbs in baptismal contexts and the emphasis he places on personal belief show that baptism refers to a particular moment of

[2]On the baptismal theology of St. Paul, see: R. Schnackenburg, *Baptism in the Thought of St. Paul* (Oxford: Blackwell, 1964). On Pauline theology generally, see G. Bornkamm, *Paul* (London: Hodder & Stoughton, 1975); W. G. Kümmel, *Theology of the New Testament*, (London: SCM, 1974), 137-254.

the past when the gospel of Jesus Christ had been preached and accepted. For Paul also, therefore, baptism belongs to the kerygmatic missionary context of the Church and represents the goal and climax of that mission. He provides evidence of a period of instruction in the christian faith before baptism, the seed of the Church's later catechumenate (Rom 6:7-8). That baptism was by a rite of immersion seems a certain implication of Romans 6:3-11. The understanding of baptism as "in the name of Jesus Christ" and thereby initiating discipleship of Christ is also familiar to Paul, as is forgiveness of sins as the sacrament's effect. (Cf. 1 Cor 1:13; 6:11; Col 1:13-14). The gift of the Spirit is a basic and important theme in Pauline theology and again the aorist verbs which he uses when referring to this gift and other associations show that there is question here of an event and effect of initiation. Here, however, as we shall see, Paul will make one of his most profound contributions in that he will integrate this gift into his understanding of baptism and thus provide a more unified concept of christian initiation than that which prevailed before him. Finally, he also emphasises that christian initiation is initiation into membership of the Church and into participation in its life and mission.

As we would have to expect, Paul is perfectly familiar with the understanding and practice of christian initiation in the primitive Church. But he is not content simply to repeat this established understanding. His concern is to develop a deeper insight into what the gospel of Christ and acceptance of that gospel means, a deeper understanding of what it means to be a Christian. In understanding this enterprise, he is involved in and committed to working out a deeper understanding of baptism and initiation than that which until then prevailed in the Church. His theological interpretation of baptism thus represents, in the words of Schnackenburg, "a marriage of the existing rite with the weighty thought of his theology."[3] The thrust of his theological endeavour in this context will be to develop and deepen the

---

[3]R. Schnackenburg, *Baptism in the Thought of St. Paul*, 30.

central christological dimension of baptism, "to put the baptized man's belonging to Christ on a deeper foundation."[4] But he also brings to this task a deep insight into what the gift of the Spirit means and involves and he thereby achieves an original integration of the christological and pneumatological dimensions of christian initiation, of the two founding, salvation events of the christian Church which underlay and determined the Church's early practice and concept of initiation.

With this introduction we may now turn to the famous passage where Paul most fully states his understanding of baptism, Romans 6:3-11, the *locus classicus* of Pauline baptismal theology. This passage will introduce us to the breadth and depth of this theology and enable us to set out the main implications of his thought.

Romans 6:3-11

This passage is the opening section of Chapter 6 of the Letter to the Romans, the most famous document of the whole Pauline corpus. It is an integral part of the whole powerful statement which this letter is. As we cannot here get involved in a commentary on Romans, we will take this passage as an entity in itself. As the verb tenses of the Greek throughout the passage are important, I indicate these in the text.

> Do you not know that all of us who have been baptized (aorist) into Christ Jesus were baptized (aorist) into his death? We were buried (aorist) therefore with him by baptism into death, so that as Christ was raised from the dead by the glory of the Father, we too might walk (subjunctive) in newness of life.
>
> For if we have been united (perfect) with him in a death like his, we shall certainly be united (future) with him in a resurrection like his. We know that our old self was

---

[4]*Ibid.*

crucified (aorist) with him so that the sinful body might be destroyed (subjunctive), and we might be no longer enslaved (purpose infinitive) to sin. For he who has died is freed (perfect) from sin. But if we have died (aorist) with Christ, we believe that we shall also live (future) with him. For we know that Christ being raised from the dead will never die again; death no longer has dominion over him. The death he died he died to sin, once for all, but the life he lives he lives to God.

So you also must consider (imperative) yourselves dead to sin and alive to God in Christ Jesus.

One's immediate impression on first reading this passage must surely be that of a crowded collection of random thoughts elbowing one another for space. The thought is certainly crowded. But, despite first impressions, it is also controlled thought, as some patient re-reading will reveal.

First, it will be helpful to note that the final statement (v. 11) is the culmination of the passage, the climax and conclusion towards which the whole piece is directed. The other statements provide the ground for this conclusion, give it its justification and motivation. Paul's main interest here, therefore, is not to be mystical or mystifying but to be utterly practical: the Christian must be dead to sin and alive to God in Jesus Christ. To explain, ground and motivate this programme of life Paul appeals to the meaning of baptism.

The different grammatical moods and tenses in the passage are significant and they indicate the shape and meaning of Paul's thought. We find indicative, subjunctive and imperative moods and in the indicative the perfect, aorist and future tenses. To deal first with the indicative tenses: the aorist, as we have said before, signifies a particular moment in past time when an action or event took place and was completed e.g. "were baptized"; the perfect refers to a state which began at some particular moment in the past but which is still continuing and is still operative here and now, e.g. "we have been united"; the future refers to a situation which is yet to be, e.g. "we shall live".

The subjunctive verbs in the passage express possibility and desirability and the imperative expresses duty. These different moods and tenses thus speak of an event of the past, a continuing state, opportunity and duty in the present, the destiny which is future. The past event is the baptism which the Roman Christians have all received, their present state is that of being baptized, of being Christian, the duty of the present is to live this state, live up to this name, the future destiny is participation in the risen glory of Christ.

Paul's purpose in this passage is very practical: to motivate the Romans to live as a christian people should, "dead to sin but alive to God in Christ Jesus." His method of doing so is to lead them to an appreciation of their christian status, of what being a Christian means. This involves him in an explanation of the meaning of baptism, the event which made them Christians. Underlying the imperative of the present and the hope of the future stands this foundation event of the past.

Paul is not content simply to repeat the old formula, baptism "in the name of Jesus Christ," with its significance of entering into relationship with Christ, becoming a disciple of Christ. His reference to being "baptized into Christ Jesus", though it is a characteristic phrase of his own, is close to the old formula, but he is anxious to probe the deeper significance of the relationship with Christ which baptism establishes. He therefore presents baptism as a dying and rising with Christ, as involving the recipient in Christ's death and resurrection. One naturally thinks here of the symbolism of immersion, of going under the water as burial in the tomb and the re-emergence as the resurrection from the tomb. But exposition by symbolism, which was to become so popular later in the Church, is not Paul's main interest here. The symbolism is secondary and subordinate. Paul's central interest is in the *meaning* of the rite, in what it represents and accomplishes rather than in what it symbolises. His main concern is to emphasise that the relationship with Christ which baptism establishes is not any mere external or juridical form of relationship but a vital union, a union which is a source of life. But this union with Christ is a union with him in the saving events of his history, his dying and rising again. So the Christian is baptized into Christ's death, "buried with him by baptism into his death", "united with him in a death like his", "crucified with him". The "death" that is in question here is not, of course, physical death, but the destruction of the "old self", "the sinful body", that is, man's subjection to the forces of evil, especially sin and physical death.

The "death" which baptism represents and accomplishes is a liberation from these forces of evil through union with Christ in his death. It is salvation. And so, since Christ's death led to his resurrection, since he, as it were, died into resurrection, so also the Christian rises with him in baptism to "newness of life" which is a participation in Christ's risen life, the life he now lives "to God", and therefore should be characterized by freedom from enslavement to sin. This state of being is the beginning and guarantee of the Christian's eventual full participation in Christ's risen glory: "if we have been united (perfect) with him in a death like his, we shall certainly be united (future) with him in a resurrection like his"; "if we have died (perfect) with Christ, we believe that we shall also live (future) with him". Thus, for the Christian the event of the past, his baptism, establishes him in a state of being which now continually urges and impels him and leads him towards his future destiny. Once this is understood, the emphasis quite naturally falls on the present, hence the practical imperative which is the climax and conclusion of the whole reflection and towards which all the energy of Paul's thought has been directed: "So you also must consider yourselves dead to sin and alive to God in Christ Jesus".

The christological emphasis in this description of the meaning of baptism is obvious and it directs us to a consideration of Paul's christology for a deeper insight into his understanding of this sacrament.

JESUS CHRIST

Paul's understanding of baptism is an integral part of his whole theology and indeed in many ways epitomises it. We have seen that in the outlook of the primitive Church, the primary and central emphasis in baptism was christological: baptism was concerned with relationship with Christ, becoming a disciple of Christ. This, too, is Paul's emphasis, but his concern is to deepen and broaden this emphasis, to bring out its depth and scope. He therefore describes the Christian's relationship with Christ established at baptism as a vital union, a union which has the power and flow of life, which is an energy that is here and now operating and impelling to growth. Christ does not exist apart from his history, the events of his life. He is what he now is because of these events, and above all because of the climaxing events of his death and resurrection. This being so, the Christian's union with Christ involves him in a union with him in his dying and rising. For Paul this throws an important light on the meaning of the Christian's being and life and his main concern is to draw out these implications. The key to Paul's baptismal theology, therefore, lies in his christology and the implications of this christology for christian life and existence.

The context to which Paul's references to baptism all belong is that of christian conversion. His major letters are written to local communities of recent converts, mainly evangelised and established by himself. In all these his concern is to strengthen and secure the conversion that was realized in the recent past when they were baptized. Paul's concept of christian conversion is determined by his understanding of the redemption of man which the victory of Christ has achieved. This redemption is the promised messianic salvation which, though already an accomplished reality, has still to be consummated and manifested in the future, at the final coming or presence of Christ, the *parousia*. The redemption of Christ has thus divided the whole of history into two periods or ages: the past where, for Jew and Gentile alike, sin reigned and man was separated from God, and the present where grace reigns because God in Christ has destroyed sin and thereby made possible man's reconciliation with Himself.

Christian conversion means passing from one age to the other, from the reign of the power of sin and death to the reign of God, the reign of life and grace. This transition has been made possible by the victory of Christ and one can enter the new era through relationship with him. Paul thus thinks in terms of historical epochs. The new epoch is under the dominion of Christ and to enter it and be part of it one must belong to Christ. Paul likes to describe this personal relationship with Christ by the use of christological prepositions, "in Christ", "with Christ", "of (=belonging to) Christ".

Paul's whole outlook is determined by his insight into what has occurred in the history of Jesus of Nazareth. This history reached its significant climax in the event of the resurrection and it is only in the light of this event that the previous history of Jesus has meaning and can be understood. The resurrection was an act of God whereby Jesus attained a transcendent status with God beyond the limitations of history, "designated Son of God in power according to the Spirit of holiness by his resurrection from the dead" (Romans 1:4). In thus breaking through the limitations of history to life with God, Jesus opens the whole of history, to which he fully belonged in his earthly life, to this same destiny. Through him the whole of history can attain to this transcendent union with God. By union with the risen Christ man shares in the status and destiny which the resurrection represents. This act of God does not terminate in the risen Christ but reaches out in him to embrace all men and the whole of history. The resurrection is thus *the* act of salvation and the risen Christ is the Savior of men.

Paul's thought is dominated by this understanding of the resurrection and the epochal victory which it represents. Here God has spoken his final word and history has already attained its transcendent destiny. This does not mean, however, that human history, with all its limitations, has ceased to exist. There was a tendency in some circles of the early Church, especially among pagan converts, to think that with christian conversion the resurrection and salvation of man had automatically occurred, that even now on earth the limitations of history were surpassed and no more. Paul was quick to spot the error in this line of thought and the danger of libertinism and antinomianism which it involved. Against this view Paul insists that only Jesus has as yet attained resurrection, that the rest of mankind remain immersed in history where God is not yet "all in all", where the forces of evil still operate and man still needs and seeks salvation. Yet the possibility of this salvation now exists because the victory of Christ has decided the fate of the powers of evil and opened human history to its ultimate destiny with God. The risen Christ is both a present factor in man's history, a saving power leading him to his destiny, and the One who has gone before and who in his risen state represents the future of man. But man still remains a prey to all the alienating forces operating in history and he must "work out his salvation in fear and trembling".

Paul thus holds in tension the finality of the resurrection and the interim, vulnerable character of human history. The Christian already possesses the promise of victory, of participation in Christ's resurrection, and the power of Christ is even now at work in him leading him to this destiny. Yet, the Christian still lives amid the limitations of history and in his daily life must work out his salvation in fear and trembling. Paul encourages the Christian to appreciate his status as being "in Christ Jesus", but at the same time he warns him he has no grounds for presumption or over-confidence. The danger, as he sees it, lies in a one-sided concentration on the event of the resurrection, as if this event could be separated from what had preceded it and the continuing flow of history which followed it. Such a concentration involved a serious misunderstanding of the resurrection itself and a serious misconception of the Christ who was raised. For the Christ who was raised was the Jesus of Nazareth who had died on the cross. Paul counters the danger he has identified by balancing a theology of resurrection with a theology of the cross.

Resurrection implies previous death, the concept otherwise is meaningless. The early christian kerygma had emphasized the identity of the Risen One and Jesus of Nazareth who had died and was buried. Paul himself knew and had preached this standard formulation. In his First Letter to the Corinthians he states:

> I would remind you, brethren, in what terms I preached to you the gospel . . . . . For I delivered to you as of first importance what I also received, that Christ died for our sins in accordance with the scriptures, that he was buried, that he was raised on the third day in accordance with the scriptures . . . . .(1 Cor 15:1, 3-4).

The resurrection of Jesus cannot be separated from his death. But neither can his death be separated from his life, because it was the logical outcome of his life, written into the logic of his life as Walter Kasper puts it.[5] It was because he had lived the life he had lived, devoting himself to the ministry of the Kingdom of God, to the service of his Abba-Father, that Jesus was executed outside the city as a common criminal. The life and death of Jesus belong together. The resurrection was the Father's vindication of the Son and his faithful service. It was the fruit of Jesus' death and life-unto-death, the definitive breakthrough to new life and new being of the One destined to be the fulfilment of God's promise to Israel. The life, death and resurrection of Jesus belong together and form a unity, a whole. Paul sees and understands this unity and realizes that it cannot be truncated into discrete parts without endangering the whole significance of Christ and his history. In his Letter to the Philippians, very probably adapting here an existing christian hymn, he expresses this unity concisely and clearly.

> He emptied himself, taking the form of a servant, being born in the likeness of men. And being found in human form he humbled himself and became obedient unto death, even death on a cross. Therefore God has highly

[5]W. Kasper, *Jesus the Christ*, (London: Burns & Oates, 1976), 67.

> exalted him and bestowed on him the name which is
> above every name, that at the name of Jesus every knee
> should bow, in heaven and on earth and under the earth,
> and every tongue confess that Jesus Christ is Lord, to the
> glory of God the Father.
>
> (Phil 2:7-11)

Paul here describes the life of Jesus as an emptying of himself, a humbling of himself, the life of a servant, an obedience unto death. These are descriptions which obviously match and echo the story of the Gospels. They capture the figure of Jesus and the road he trod. This is the form of life which issues in resurrection, of which resurrection is the fruit.

The implications of this christology, of this fusion of a theology of resurrection and a theology of the cross, for the Pauline theology of baptism should now be plain. In and by his baptism the Christian is united to Jesus Christ so that now he is "in Christ", sharing in Christ's being. He has thereby entered and become part of the pattern which is the history of Jesus. As Jesus' road to his destiny of glory was by way of the cross, by his obedience unto death, so too must it be for the Christian. He too is committed from his baptism to travelling this road. There are no short cuts to resurrection. He is committed to the struggle of life dedicated to God, "alive to God". This is his obedience unto death, his way of the cross, which, because of his union with Christ, is acceptable to the Father and will bear the fruit of his ultimate participation in the resurrection of Jesus Christ.

The crowded thoughts of Paul's great exposition of baptism in Romans 6:3-11 now fall more clearly into place. Baptism means being united with Jesus Christ according to the pattern of his history. One is united with him in his death and resurrection. Union with him in his death signifies the end or death of the old self, the being that belonged to the old epoch dominated by the powers of evil. This very death is a liberation which ushers in the new state, "the newness of life", the life that should be free from enslavement to sin, the life for God. This is not yet resurrection; that remains, in the interim of continuing human history, still future promise. But the promise is secure in the resurrection of Christ and the liberated new life is already a reflection of that future glory.

The Spirit of Christ

Throughout Paul's exposition of the meaning of baptism in Romans 6, there is no mention of the gift of the Spirit. This silence, however, cannot be regarded as significant, because in accordance with the way he planned this document Paul reserves this theme for a later place, Chapter 8. The Spirit of God is, in fact, a major theme in the Pauline theology. Paul knows and uses the special Spirit-terminology of the New Testament: the Spirit is "given", "poured out", "received"; the Christian is "anointed", "sealed" with the Spirit. Once again, the verb tenses, aorist and perfect indicative, show that reception of the Spirit occurred at some definite point of time in the past and remains a continuing condition.[6] Reception of the Spirit, therefore, is an event of christian initiation. But Paul, in contrast here with the practice and thought of the primitive Church, associates the giving of the Spirit much more with the rite of baptism: "You were washed, you were sanctified, you were justified in the name of the Lord Jesus Christ and in the Spirit of our God" (1 Cor 6:11); "for by one Spirit we were all baptized into one body.....and all were imbued with (were made to drink of: RSV) one Spirit" (1 Cor 12:13). Together with the fact that Paul nowhere mentions imposition of hands as an initiation rite, or any post-baptismal rite, this has led many scholars to assert that Paul knows nothing of any rite for the giving of the Spirit other than baptism. This conclusion, however, is over-hasty. Certainly there is a shift of perspective on this matter in Paul in comparison with the position evidenced by the Acts of the Apostles. But the reason for this lies in Paul's concept and theology of the Spirit, which is distinctive and shows a significant development on the understanding of the Spirit then and later

[6] *1 Cor* 6:11; 12:13; *2 Cor* 1:21-22; *Rom* 5:5; 8:15; *Ephes* 1:13; *Tit* 3:5-6.

prevailing in the early Church. The first step towards appreciating the place of the Spirit in Paul's understanding of baptism must be to identify and outline this theology of the Spirit.

The concept of the Spirit which prevailed in mainstream Judaism at the time of Christ was as the Spirit of prophecy. This was the concept which the early Church inherited and it was in terms of this concept that it understood and presented the Spirit active in its own life. The Spirit of Pentecost, the Spirit which filled the Church and was received in christian initiation, was the prophetic Spirit. According to this concept, which was the classic concept of the Spirit of Yahweh in the Old Testament, the Spirit was the source of divine revelation, of the irruption of God's word among men. Accordingly, the characteristic marks of this Spirit were powerful preaching and the extraordinary signs which accompanied and confirmed this preaching. One can see this concept very clearly in St. Luke's presentation of Jesus and his ministry in his Gospel — the inspired preaching accompanied and confirmed by the miraculous activity, all "in the power of the Spirit" (Luke 4:14; cf. 4:18-21). It is the same concept of the Spirit which meets us in St. Luke's second volume, Acts, which describes the life of the early Church. The Spirit active in the Church from Pentecost on is a continuation and extension of the Spirit active in the ministry of Jesus. The same type of phenomena again manifest the Spirit's presence, powerful preaching, extraordinary signs (e.g. Acts 2). This is the Spirit of prophecy, the fulfilment of the prophecy of Joel, that has been poured out upon the Church.

St. Paul, too, is familiar with this concept of the prophetic Spirit. This was the prevailing concept of the Spirit in his own Judaism and in the new community he joined after his experience on the road to Damascus. This also was the power active in his own extraordinary missionary activity. "When I came to you, brethren", he writes to his Corinthian converts, "I did not come proclaiming to you the testimony of God in lofty words or wisdom.....my speech and my message were not in plausible words or wisdom, but in demonstration of the Spirit and power" (1 Cor 2:1, 4). This was the Spirit which he saw manifest itself in the new communities he established, in the extraordinary or charismatic gifts which became so prominent a feature of their existence (1 Cor 12). But the disruptive tendency of these phenomena also posed problems for Paul and forced him to reflect deeply on the meaning of the Spirit of God so abundantly present in the Church. 1 Corinthians 12-14 is obviously the fruit of this reflection. But Paul's restless, searching mind continued to probe this theme. He had come to recognise that the risen Christ represented and fulfilled the promised new creation foretold by the prophets and that the Christian, being "in Christ", was part of this new creation (Gal 6:14; 2 Cor 5:17). This notion of the new creation recalls the role of the *life-giving* Spirit in the Old Testament, the agent of the first creation and in the prophets the agent again of the new creation. The carefully thought out allusion to Ezechiel 36:26-27 and 37 (the Vision of the Dry Bones) in 2 Corinthians 3, shows Paul's consciousness of this background. He has identified the Spirit poured out on the Church as the *life-giving* Spirit, the agent and force of the new creation established by the resurrection of Christ: "the Spirit gives life" (2 Cor 3:6).

Once Paul has got his concept of the life-giving Spirit, he is able to apply and use this concept christologically and thus open up a whole new vista to the christian understanding. If the Spirit is the agent of the new creation and if this new creation is established in the resurrection of Jesus, then the Spirit is the divine power which raises Jesus to this new life and establishes him in his exalted state. The opening verses of the Letter to the Romans reveals his thought.

> Paul, a servant of Jesus Christ, called to be an apostle, set apart for the gospel of God, which he promised beforehand through his prophets in the holy scriptures, the gospel concerning his Son, who was descended from David according to the flesh and designated Son of God in power according to the Spirit of holiness by his resurrection from the dead, Jesus Christ our Lord. . . . . (Rom 1:1-4).

The earthly Jesus, Jesus "according to the flesh", is established in power in his resurrection by the Spirit of God. He is now so penetrated by God's Spirit, God's very being, that Paul feels entitled to say: "the last Adam (i.e. Christ) became a life-giving Spirit" (1 Cor 15:45). The Spirit of God is now, therefore, the Spirit of Christ, the Spirit of the Lord (Rom 8:9; 2 Cor 3:17-18), Whoever is united to Christ thereby shares in this Spirit which, as the Spirit of Christ, is the Spirit of Sonship of God (Rom 8:14-17). For Paul union with Christ and possession of the Spirit are the one thing, because the Spirit is the Spirit of Christ. Men become part of the new creation, enter the new and final epoch of the messianic blessings, by receiving the promised Spirit of God. This Spirit is now available through union with the risen Christ. United with Christ and sharing in his Spirit they now have operating in them the life-giving power of Christ's Spirit. This power, if they but open themselves to its influence, will enable them to triumph over the forces of evil still operating in history and will lead them to their final destiny which is full participation in Christ's resurrection and eternal life with God.

The full force of the theological synthesis Paul has here achieved is best appreciated, not by any further exposition, but from his own words in Romans 8, the *locus classicus* of his theology of the Spirit, as chapter 6 is of his baptismal theology. The two passages, indeed, are complementary and belong together.

> There is therefore now no condemnation for those who are in Christ Jesus. For the law of the Spirit of life in Christ Jesus has set me free from the law of sin and death. For God has done what the law, weakened by the flesh, could not do: sending his own Son in the likeness of sinful flesh and for sin, he condemned sin in the flesh, in order that the just requirement of the law might be fulfilled in us, who walk not according to the flesh but according to the Spirit. For those who live according to the flesh set their minds on the things of the flesh, but those who live according to the Spirit, set their minds on the things of

the Spirit. To set the mind on the flesh is death, but to set the mind on the Spirit is life and peace. For the mind that is set on the flesh is hostile to God; it does not submit to God's law, indeed it cannot; and those who are in the flesh cannot please God.

But you are not in the flesh, you are in the Spirit, if the Spirit of God really dwells in you. Anyone who does not have the Spirit of Christ does not belong to him. But if Christ is in you, although your bodies are dead because of sin, your spirits are alive because of righteousness. If the Spirit of him who raised Christ Jesus from the dead dwells in you, he who raised Christ Jesus from the dead will give life to your mortal bodies also through his Spirit which dwells in you.

So then, brethren, we are debtors, not to the flesh, to live according to the flesh—for if you live according to the flesh you will die, but if by the Spirit you put to death the deeds of the body you will live. For all who are led by the Spirit of God are sons of God. For you did not receive the spirit of slavery to fall back into fear, but you have received the spirit of sonship. When we cry 'Abba! Father!' it is the Spirit himself bearing witness with our spirit that we are children of God, and if children, then heirs, heirs of God and fellow heirs with Christ, provided we suffer with him in order that we may also be glorified with him.

(Romans 8:1-17)

Many themes and expressions here hark back to and re-echo parallel themes and expressions in the earlier passage from Romans 6. There Paul had spoken of a vital union with Christ, of death to sin and life for God, of future resurrection. This passage speaks likewise of death to sin, life for God and resurrection, but now the source of all this is the Spirit of Christ dwelling in the Christian. The intimate relation Paul has established between Christ and the Spirit, made possible by his retrieval of the concept of the life-giving Spirit, is the reason for this coincidence. But the position to which Paul's insights has led him has obvious implications for his understanding of christian initiation. In the early thinking of the Church, Christ and the Spirit are independent, though closely related, concepts and the primitive Church's practice and understanding of christian initiation reflect this. Once Paul has achieved his theological breakthrough by integrating these concepts, this old understanding of initiation is, for him, inevitably implicated and affected.

In the early practice of christian initiation the christological and pneumatological references are separated into two distinct rites, baptism and imposition of hands. No doubt, by the time Paul is writing his major letters, between 50 and 60 A.D., these rites already form one somewhat complex ceremony, as Acts 19:1-7 suggests and Hebrews 6:2 further confirms. Paul by his very intimate relation of Christ and the Spirit has integrated these two references and thereby has transcended the old understanding. For him now these two go and belong *together*. Paul is not satisfied to speak of baptism simply as establishing relationship with Christ, no matter how personal one conceives this. He is not satisfied simply to repeat the old formula "baptism in the name of Jesus Christ". He wishes to speak, and does speak, of a *union* with Christ, a vital union, a union of being which is a source of life. He wishes to give relationship with Christ an ontological basis and meaning. But granting his fusion together, though never to the point of absolute identification, of Christ and the Spirit, this union with Christ, which is established in baptism, must also involve receiving the Spirit of Christ, the Spirit of God. One simply cannot be united with Christ without sharing in his Spirit. For Paul, therefore, the gift of the Spirit is already involved in the union with Christ established in baptism.

What are the implications of this Pauline theology as regards the post-baptismal rite of imposition of hands for the giving of the Spirit? Paul does not mention this rite and many scholars have seen this silence as significant, that is, that he did not know of the existence of the rite. This, in turn, obliges them to cast doubt on the references to this rite in the Acts of the Apostles and to seek a solution to the problem thus created other than the obvious one of accepting Acts at its face value. On this issue it must be bluntly stated that the silence of Paul cannot be made to bear the weight of this interpretation. Paul, as we have noted, is not interested in sacramental rites as liturgical ceremonies. Even his references to baptism are incidental. His interest in sacraments is their meaning and especially their practical implications. His references to them are incidental to his doctrinal and practical interests. Further, he is far from hostile to the established traditions of the Church, rather he upholds them.

His originality consists in his theological and intellectual insights. This is the key to the issue in question here. Paul's theological system is an organic whole; upset one part of this unity and the whole is disrupted. Once he has integrated the concepts of discipleship of Christ and the gift of the Spirit, he cannot conveniently parcel out these effects chronologically to separate rites. His theology precludes him from doing so. He has to integrate the gift of the Spirit with the union with Christ which is achieved in baptism. But this does not at all mean that he suppressed the other rite on his own initiative. Nothing in his way of acting suggests he would take such a liberty. How he envisaged this rite, in view of his new theology, we have no means of knowing, since he simply does not inform us.

I would think it probable that he saw baptism and imposition of hands as two expressions of the one reality. Certainly in planning his *Letter to the Romans* he found himself obliged to discuss the two themes in separate sections, and this may be an indication of his mind. He would not have had in this situation our somewhat rationalistic concept of a chronological sequence to sacramental effects. But it is his theological insights and understanding which above all explains his lack of reference to the post-baptismal rite. His concept of the life-giving Spirit and his application of this concept logically obliges him, in his references to christian initiation, to associate this gift with the union with Christ established in baptism. What is nowadays called the problem of confirmation has its source here in this theologically correct intuition of Paul. Writers who seek this source in later developments, when the problem explicitly manifests itself, are therefore following a wrong trail.

Baptism and the Christian

Paul's main interest in all his references to baptism is supremely practical: to motivate the Christian to live his faith. Baptism is the source of christian existence and life. The meaning of baptism therefore reveals the meaning of christian existence and provides the motivation for living the christian faith and life. In his discussion of baptism Paul emphasises a number of basic themes or dimensions in which the meaning of the sacrament consists. His understanding of baptism is an organic whole formed by these themes, a building constructed by these bricks and mortar. The significance of baptism for christian existence and life, for being a christian, is disclosed in these its basic dimensions. From the beginning christian initiation consisted of two basic references, Christ and the gift of the Spirit. These remain basic and central also for Paul. But he probes and applies the deeper implications of these aspects more profoundly than any other writer of the New Testament. His reflection leads him to develop those themes which form his baptismal theology. We can grasp the overall shape of his thought by outlining these basic dimensions of baptism and their significance in the life of the Christian.

CONVERSION

As we have mentioned earlier, the context of Paul's thought on baptism is that of conversion. Paul thinks of history as consisting of two epochs, the first where the forces of evil, expecially sin and death, hold sway and the second where the dominion of these forces, even though they continue to exist, has been broken and the grace of God reigns. He thinks of these epochs in terms of the persons who initiated them and constitute their source. The old epoch of fallen humanity has its source in Adam and his sin: "Sin came into the world through one man and death through sin, and so death spread to all men because all men sinned" (Rom 5:12). The new epoch has its source in Jesus Christ and the redemption he accomplished: "if many died through one man's trespass, much more have the grace of God and the free gift in the grace of that one man Jesus Christ abounded for many" (Rom 5:15); "for as by one man's disobedience many were made sinners, so by one man's obedience many will be made righteous" (Rom 5:19). Paul is applying here the semitic and biblical concept of corporate personality. According to this concept the head or leader of a group, such as the father of the family or the king of the nation, incorporated in himself and expressed in himself the whole group so that they formed one being in him. The head, as it were, constituted a mode of being, an energy-field as we might describe it today, which penetrated and embraced the whole group.

This notion is the source of Paul's concept of the two epochs of history, the two modes of being which define man and his life, and this too is the source of his Adam-Christ contrast which sums up for him his understanding of salvation history (cf. Rom 5; 1 Cor 15:21-22). Adam and Christ each constitute a mode of being for man, the one of enslavement to the forces of evil, the other of liberation from these forces for life and union with God. "As by a man came death, by a man has come also the resurrection of the dead. For as in Adam all die, so also in Christ shall all be made alive" (1 Cor 15:21-22).

For Paul all men by birth are part of fallen humanity, they belong to Adam. To escape from this condition they must come to know and acknowledge Jesus Christ and be united with hm. This transition is christian conversion and it is accomplished in baptism. Baptism is the point of transition from the domain of Adam with all it represents to that of Christ and what he constitutes and represents. This is a mode of being in the life-giving Spirit of God. By baptism the Christian enters and becomes part of this divine mode of being. He exists now in Christ and in the Spirit of God. This, however, does not mean that the need for effort and struggle in life is over. The new epoch constituted by Christ and his victory has not yet attained its ultimate consummation which is the resurrection of man with Christ. This is still future, it remains destiny. Meanwhile, the evil forces of the old epoch continue to exist and affect the lives of men. But their power and dominion has been broken and the Christian through God's grace, through his life in Christ and the Spirit, is able to resist and overcome them. His conversion and baptism commit him to this struggle, the struggle of the christian life. If this effort is forthcoming, this dying with Christ, then the destiny of also rising with him is secure.

> For as in Adam all die, so also in Christ shall all be made alive. But each in his own order: Christ the first fruits, then at his coming those who belong to Christ. Then comes the end, when he delivers the kingdom to God the Father after destroying every rule and every authority and power. For he must reign until he has put all his enemies under his feet. The last enemy to be destroyed is death. . . . . When all things are subjected to him, then the Son himself will also be subjected to him who put all things under him, that God may be everything to everyone.
>
> 1 Cor 15:22-26, 28.

THE TRINITY

The thrust of Paul's thought in his analysis of the status of the Christian is to go beyond a concept of a merely external relationship between Christ and the Christian and to attempt to conceive this relationship at a deeper level, an ontological level, as a state of being. He speaks in terms of union with Christ, of the Christian being "in Christ", of life through Christ. The Christian shares in Christ's mode of being. Since this mode of being is divine, it is constituted and exhausted by the Father, the Son and the Spirit. This enables Paul to conceive the Christian's state of being in trinitarian and personal terms. The Christian shares in the divine relationships which constitute the being of God.

The Christian enters into these relationships through his union with Christ and his endowment with the Spirit of Christ which establishes that union. Since the status of Christ is most accurately described by the title the Son of God, union with Christ means for the Christian participation in this sonship in the Spirit.

> When the time had fully come, God sent forth his Son, born of woman, born under the law, to redeem those who were under the law, so that we might receive adoption as sons. And because you are sons, God has sent the Spirit of his Son into our hearts, crying: 'Abba! Father'.
>
> (Gal 4:4-6)

Christians are the adopted sons of God in Christ and in the Spirit. Participating in this sonship, they share in Christ's own relationship with the Father and can address him with Christ's own intimate form of address: Abba! God has communicated himself, opened his very life, to men through Christ in the Spirit: "God was in Christ reconciling the world to himself" (2 Cor 5:19). Sharing in Christ's relationship with the Father means for the Christian sharing also in Christ's ordination of his life to the Father. The Father was the source from which Christ lived, from which he was "sent forth", and the Father likewise was the centre to which he dedicated himself and devoted his life, "he emptied himself, taking the form of a servant, ... he humbled himself and became obedient unto death, even death on a cross" (Phil 2:7-8). Union with Christ involves the Christian in this same direction of life. He, too, receives all from God the Father, "God, who in Christ always leads us in triumph" (2 Cor 2:14). And he, too, like Christ, must render his whole being and life to God: "I appeal to you therefore, brethren, to present your bodies as a living sacrifice, holy and acceptable to God, which is your spiritual worship" (Rom 12:1). The Christian must be "alive to God in Christ Jesus" (Rom 6:11).

The basic gift which the Christian receives from God through his union with Christ and the source of all other gifts and blessings, is the gift of the Holy Spirit: "God's love has been poured into our hearts through the Holy Spirit which has been given to us". (Rom 5:5). It is in the power of this Spirit that the Christian is united to Christ and enabled to direct his life to God: "All who are led by the Spirit of God are sons of God.....You have received the Spirit of sonship. When we cry, 'Abba! Father!', it is the Spirit himself bearing witness with our spirit that we are children of God, and if children, then heirs, heirs of God and fellow heirs with Christ, provided we suffer with him in order that we may also be glorified with him" (Rom 8:14-17).

One may sum up Paul's thought by saying that God is Trinity, Father, Son and Holy Spirit. To be united to God means being given a share in these relationships. This is accomplished in baptism where we are united with Christ and come to share his relationship with the Father in the Spirit. This is the trinitarian dimension of baptism and christian initiation, of existence "in Christ" and "in the Spirit". In Ephesians 2:18, Paul (or the Pauline author) sums it up in terms of access to God: "Through him (Christ) we both (Jew and Gentile) have access in the one Spirit to the Father".

INCORPORATION INTO THE CHURCH

From the beginning in early Christianity christian initiation was understood as admission to membership of the Church and participation in its life. Paul also has this understanding, but his deeper reflection on the meaning of Christ and the Spirit leads him to a more profound concept of Church and of the relation between baptism and Church.

For early christianity, to which Paul emphatically belongs, the Church of Christ was the true People of God, the true Israel. It was therefore in full continuity with the history of Israel and its people, the people formed by God into a royal priesthood for worship through the election and faith of Abraham and the events of the Exodus under Moses. But this history of Israel had been Promise looking forward to Fulfilment. This Fulfilment had now occurred in the event of Jesus the Christ, and Jesus' disciples who acknowledged him as the Christ and had received the Spirit were now the true Israel, the true People of God, the People of the End Time. They quickly came to recognise their distinctiveness and their independence from Judaism. Fulfilment had ushered in a new era which surpassed and transcended the old and brought liberation from its institutions and prescriptions which were now obsolete. All men, Jew and Gentile alike, could become part of this community and its life on an equal basis.

For the christian community the great founder figures of Israel, Abraham and Moses, belonged to the period of promise which was now surpassed. Their founder and leader was Jesus Christ, the Lord, the Son of God. They formed the community of Christ's disciples. Paul's concept of the Christian's union with Christ, of his being "in Christ", sharing in his life in the Spirit, led him to formulate a deeper understanding of the Church than that conveyed by an external fellowship. If Christians were united to Christ, then they were united with one another in Christ, they formed one vital organism, one body in Christ and shared in the one life. In this way Paul gradually developed and sharpened his concept of the Church as the Body of Christ and Temple of the Holy Spirit. (Rom 12:4-6; 1 Cor 12:12-28; Col 1:18-19; Eph 4:12-16; 1 Cor 3:16; 6:19-20). United to Christ, Christians formed one body with him and lived from his life.

Since baptism constitutes initiation into the Church, Paul incorporates baptism into his new vision of the Church. He finds a parallel between the waters of the sea through which the people of Israel passed to freedom and the waters of baptism. The one prefigures and is fulfilled in the other. Baptism is the way to true and ultimate freedom, establishing the people of the true exodus, the true and final People of God (1 Cor 10:1-4, 11). It is baptism which brings into existence and establishes the People of God of the End Time. This people is a community united to God through Christ in the Spirit (Eph 2:18). The true People of God are the Church, the Body of Christ, the people formed through union with Christ in his Spirit. Since it is in baptism that one is united to Christ, incorporated into Christ (Rom 6:3-11) and receives his Spirit, so also in baptism one is incorporated into the Church, the Body of Christ, and united in that Body with all its other members. The Church is a body animated by the Spirit of Christ. Through baptism one becomes a member of that body and animated by its Spirit.

> Just as the body is one and has many members, and all the members of the body, though many, are one body, so it is with Christ. For by one Spirit we were all baptized into one body—Jews or Greeks, slave or free—and all were imbued with (made to drink of, RSV) one Spirit.
>
> (1 Cor 12:12-13)

> For as many of you as were baptized into Christ have put on Christ. There is neither Jew nor Greek, there is neither slave nor free, there is neither male nor female, for you are all one in Christ Jesus. And if you are Christ's then you are Abraham's offspring, heirs according to the promise.....When the time had fully come, God sent forth his Son, born of woman, born under the law, to redeem those who were under the law, so that we might receive adoption as sons. And because you are sons, God has sent the Spirit of his Son into our hearts, crying, 'Abba! Father!' So through God you are no longer a slave but a son, and if a son then an heir'.
>
> (Gal 3:27-29; 4:4-7).

Paul carries over into his concept of the Church the depth he came to recognise in the Christian's relationship with Christ. If the individual Christian is "in Christ", is in vital contact with Christ's divine state of being, then all Christians together form one body, one vital organism with Christ and with one another in Christ. We have seen how Paul's concept of the Spirit as the life-giving Spirit of Christ helped him to formulate this understanding of the Christian's union with Christ and to integrate into a coherent unity the notions of discipleship of Christ and possession of the Spirit. The extension to the Church as a whole of this concept of the Christian's union with Christ in the Spirit is an easy and a logical step for Paul. The whole community of Christians is a body united with Christ and animated by his

Spirit. What is true of the individual Christian is true of the body of Christians, the Church. If baptism represents and effects incorporation into Christ, it also in this one act represents and effects incorporation into the Church, the Body of Christ and Temple of the Holy Spirit. If the People of God of the old era were formed as such by passing through the waters of the sea, so now the final People of God, the community of Christ, are formed by passing through the waters of baptism. Baptism for Paul has a strong community and ecclesial significance.

> When the goodness and loving kindness of God our Saviour appeared, he saved us, not because of deeds done by us in righteousness, but in virtue of his own mercy, by the washing of regeneration and renewal in the Holy Spirit, which he poured out upon us richly through Jesus Christ our Saviour, so that we might be justified by his grace and become heirs in hope of eternal life. (Tit 3:4-7).

For the Christian and the Church, baptism means birth to new life in Christ and in his Spirit.

THE LIFE OF THE CHRISTIAN

Paul's purpose in all his writings, as we have often insisted, is practical. The christian communities he had established were composed of recent converts, many of them from paganism with little or no knowledge of or training in Jewish religious thought and practice. Their conversion committed them to living a new and difficult way of life in a pagan world amid old associations. Paul fully realizes the difficulties and in his letters he seeks both to instruct these converts to what the christian life demands and to motivate and encourage them to live up to these ideals. This is the practical purpose which always underlies his deep theological reflection. He is not content simply to state the practical demands of christian life, he seeks to explain the basic reasons which form the foundation of the christian ethic. His basic principle is that the christian life is a living out of the christian state, the christian condition of being and existence. The principle could be summed up in the words: Become what you are. Paul's purpose is to explain to the Christian what he or she is as a way of encouraging and motivating them to live their state. He likes to insist on this coherence of state of being and life. Addressing the Corinthians in his first letter he speaks of them as "those sanctified in Christ Jesus" and yet also as "called to be saints" (1 Cor 1:2). He addresses the Romans in the words: "To all God's beloved in Rome, who are called to be saints" (Rom 1:7). To the Ephesians he (or the Pauline author in his name) appeals: "I beg you to lead a life worthy of the calling to which you have been called" (Eph 4:1).

It is supremely important to Paul, therefore, that the Christian realize his state, who and what he is. We have seen that he defines this state in trinitarian and therefore in personal terms. The Christian is one related to God the Father as son or daughter through Christ in the Spirit. This relationship, then, is the condition which the Christian must live out in his or her life. His being and life must be directed *to* the Father.

> I appeal to you, brethren, to present your bodies as a living sacrifice, holy and acceptable to God, which is your spiritual worship (Rom 12:1).

> Whether you eat or drink, or whatever else you do, do all to the glory of God (1 Cor 10:31).

Put more briefly, the Christian must be "alive to God" (Rom 6:11).

This direction of life to God is not something the Christian can accomplish of himself, out of his own will. He can live this life simply because he has received it, it has been given to him, it is a gift, a grace. This theme is so basic to Paul's thought that it is pointless to attempt to document it. It is the message of every line he wrote. The Christian receives this life from God the Father through Christ in the Spirit. The existence of the Christian, the christian state, is founded on and established by God's communication of himself to him in Christ and in the Spirit. To live that state means living with Christ, in union with him, in the power of the Spirit. Once again we return to the double reference of christian initiation, the reference to relationship with Christ and the reference to the gift of the Holy Spirit. The imperative which dominates and motivates christian living is the imperative to live this state of being. Since Paul has integrated these two references, he can express this imperative as it suits him in terms of either. But his basic principle of christian living is the same: the Christian must live a life in imitation of Christ; the Christian must live a life led by the Spirit of God.

To borrow the useful concept of Newman's, Paul's understanding of the Christian's state as being in Christ, of being united to Christ, is no mere notional one, it is real: "I have been crucified with Christ; it is no longer I who live, but Christ lives in me" (Gal 2:20). This is no mere general principle but a personal, experiential statement which is obscured rather than clarified by the label mysticism. It is simply a statement of Paul's strong sense of his own union in and with Jesus Christ. It is also an ethical principle: "to me to live is Christ" (Phil 1:21). Paul urges on his fellow-Christians this same personal sense of union with Christ and a corresponding life in imitation of Christ.

> Do you not realise that Jesus Christ is in you
>
>   (2 Cor 13:5).
>
> .....the glory of this mystery, which is Christ in us, the hope of glory.
>
>   (Col 1:27)
>
> Christ is all, and in all.
>
>   (Col 3:11).
>
> Have this mind among yourselves which you have in Christ Jesus.
>
>   (Phil 2:5).
>
> Be imitators of me, as I am of Christ.
>
>   (1 Cor 11:1; cf. 1 Cor 4:16; 1 Thess 1:6).

This imitation of Christ which is the struggle of the christian life is what Paul means by his concept of dying with Christ, a dying which can be achieved only through the power of the risen Christ living in the Christian.

Since for Paul union with Christ and being indwelt by his Spirit amount to the one thing, he can also state this christian ethic in terms of the gift of the Spirit. Since the Spirit is God's gift to and in the Christian, the Christian does not determine of himself what the Spirit says to him. His role is one of submission to the lead and promptings of the Spirit. The Christian is "alive to God" because the life-giving Spirit of God, which is also the Spirit of Christ, is in him, animating him. Therefore, in his life the Christian must allow himself to be led by the Spirit.

> If you live according to the flesh you will die, but if by the Spirit, you put to death the deeds of the body, you will live. All who are led by the Spirit of God are sons of God. For you did not receive the spirit of slavery to fall back into fear, but you have received the spirit of sonship.
> (Rom 8:13-15).

> For the law of the Spirit of life in Christ Jesus has set me free from the law of sin and death.
> (Rom 8:2)

This road along which the Spirit leads the Christian is the life of christian charity. This life, which Paul describes so vividly in 1 Corinthians 13, has its source and sustaining power in God's gift of the life-giving Spirit: "God's love has been poured into our hearts through the Holy Spirit which has been given to us" (Rom 5:5). The life of christian charity is the achievement of the Spirit of Christ working in the Christian. In Galatians 5:25 Paul states his principle clearly and succinctly:

> If we live by the Spirit, let us also walk by the Spirit

This "walking by the Spirit" will then issue in "the fruit of the Spirit", those personal qualities which should characterise the person and life of the Christian.

> The fruit of the Spirit is love, joy, peace, patience, kindness, goodness, faithfulness, gentleness, self-control; against such there is no law.
>
> (Gal 5:22-23).

For Paul, then, the christian life is a living out of the christian state. St. Thomas Aquinas summed up the principle in his terse manner: *vivere est esse*: life is being in action. Since the Christian enters this state through baptism, since it is in this sacramental event that he comes to exist "in Christ" and "in the Spirit" and is given access to the Father, his baptism launches him on this programme of life and commits him to living his life after the manner of Jesus Christ and in the power of the Spirit. In this sense baptism is the source of the christian life and the christian life is a continual living out of one's baptism.

> We were buried therefore with him by baptism into death, so that as Christ was raised from the dead by the glory of the Father, we too might walk in newness of life.
>
> (Rom 6:4)

BAPTISM AND ETERNAL LIFE

Paul's concept of the two epochs of history, the old and the new, was open to the misconception that for the Christian the new era had totally succeeded the old, that the old no longer existed, the End-Time had fully come. If this were the case, the Christian now was already fully risen with Christ, the future held nothing further for him, and even Christ's own resurrection would now have to be conceived in similar terms to that of the Christian and thereby be totally reduced. In this understanding any concept of the necessity for the moral effort of the christian life lost all point. Life was totally reduced to the immutable state of being and all moral striving was rendered redundant.

Paul continually corrected this misunderstanding and warded off its challenge by emphasising the reality and transcendence of Jesus' resurrection (1 Cor 15:1-19) and that the Christian did not yet fully share this state of glory with Christ (1 Cor 15:20-58). The risen Christ is "the first fruits of those who have fallen asleep" (1 Cor 15:20). The rest of the harvest has yet to be saved.

> For as in Adam all die, so also in Christ shall (future) all be made alive. But each in his own order: Christ the first fruits, then at his coming those who belong to Christ.
>
> (1 Cor 15:22-23. Cf. Rom 6:8)

The Christian's resurrection with Christ still remains a future destiny. For the present he lives in a "between times" where the old and the new orders co-exist. But the power of the old order, the power of the forces of evil, of sin and death especially, has been broken by the redemption of Christ and the grace of God in Christ and his Spirit which that redemption has made available. Living in the new order through his being in Christ, the Christian must conquer in himself through God's grace the power of the Old order which still afflicts him. This struggle of the christian life is a necessary condition for attaining the future destiny, the final consummation of sharing in Christ's resurrection and glory. Since this destiny means full participation in Christ's risen state, it only belongs to those who are "in Christ". The Christian must therefore maintain his state of being "in Christ", entered at baptism, if he is to attain this destiny which his being in Christ promises him. This maintaining of existence in Christ is the christian life. The imperative of the christian life, then, is not merely a duty stemming from a commitment undertaken in the past, when the Christian was united with Christ in baptism. It is also an imperative from the future, a calling of the destiny which awaits the Christian who is true to his name and status.

Christian existence and life is thus eschatological, directed to an end in the future and determined by that end. Paul brings past, present and future into a coherent unity. The past is established in the event of Christ and the gift of the Spirit and the Christian's participation in these events through his entry into the Church at baptism. The present should be a living out of this existence in Christ and in the

Spirit begun in baptism. The future is the full flowering of this past maintained in the continuing present, the Harvest-Home. For those who remain faithful, this future is secure, since it is the promise of God himself and is under-written by him in Christ and in the gift of the Spirit: "If we have died with Christ, we believe we shall also live with him" (Rom 6:4): "God has put his seal upon us and given us his Spirit in our hearts as a guarantee" (2 Cor 1:22).

The Christian's orientation to eternal life is the very meaning of his existence in Christ. His union with Christ and possession of the Spirit is the beginning of this life, "the first fruits of the Spirit" (Rom 8:23). As it is in baptism that he was first united to Christ and received his Spirit, so it was in his baptism that he was given his destiny and received the promise and guarantee of eternal life. His baptism was a seal, a sealing of God in his gift of the Spirit "for the day of redemption" (Ephes 4:30; cf. 2 Cor 1:22; Ephes 1:13). The Christian was baptized with a view to eternal life and his baptism continually directs him towards this end.

> We know that the whole creation has been groaning in travail together until now; and not only the creation, but we ourselves, who have the first fruits of the Spirit, groan inwardly as we wait for adoption as sons, the redemption of our bodies. For in this hope we were saved (Rom 8:22-24).

Conclusion

Paul inherited the early Church's understanding of christian initiation with its double reference to discipleship of Christ and the gift of the Holy Spirit. Discipleship he conceives as union with Christ, a participation in his divine state of being in the "between-times" and also a pledge of full participation in Christ's risen glory in the future. His concept of the Spirit as the life-giving Spirit enables him to integrate this gift with his notion of the Christian's union with Christ. The Spirit is the Spirit of Christ and union with

Christ involves sharing in his Spirit. This theological insight integrates the two aspects of christian initiation which the early Church had associated with its two rites of baptism and imposition of hands. There is no evidence that Paul dispensed with this latter rite but there is no doubt his interest is focused on baptism. It is his theological development which has determined this focus. This theology does not require of him distinct reference to the post-baptismal rite and in fact such a reference might only prove an embarrassment in that it could tend to disrupt the close integration of Christ and the Spirit which this theology has achieved.

The christological and pneumatological references of christian initiation remain basic for Paul, but his integration and deeper understanding of these enable him to weave together into a coherent tapestry the various themes and dimensions which initiation exhibits. Since in this context baptism dominates his thought, baptism for him is an event of profound significance which, when its implications are unfolded, discloses the meaning of christian existence and life in all its breadth and depth. The Church will not surpass this understanding of baptism but will ever return to it for enlightenment and inspiration.

> There is one body and one Spirit, just as you were called to the one hope that belongs to your call, one Lord, one faith, one baptism, one God and Father of us all, who is above all and through all and in all.
>
> (Eph 4, 4-6)

Part II
Initiation in the Life of the Church

Chapter Six

RITE AND CEREMONY

Ritual as Expression

Sacraments are statements, but in a manner peculiar to themselves; they are actions, but a special kind of action. They are not theoretical statements, not even doctrinal statements, though they are full of doctrinal implications and doctrinal statements may be made about them. They constitute a special form of human activity known as ritual. Ritual is symbolic religious activity. Its essence is the symbolic re-enactment of some religious event which the participant by his participation in the symbolic act personally experiences and shares in. In the case of christian sacraments, the religious event is the living reality of Christ who constitutes the life of the christian community. It is the christian community, the Church, which performs the christian sacraments and in this ritual it celebrates its life and thereby strengthens this life for itself and its participating members. Without this sacramental celebration the christian community would not continue to exist, at least not in any form true to its historical identity. The eucharist is the primary christian sacrament and the clearest example of what such a sacrament is. In its sacraments of initiation the Church again celebrates the reality which is its life, Jesus Christ and the gift of the Spirit, and opens this life to new members.

The celebration of a sacrament consists of interconnected words and symbolic actions which together constitute the ritual of the sacrament. Though modern civilization is not as familiar with or conscious of ritual as the ancient world, it still remains a basic form of human activity and expression. It is most evident on ceremonial occasions, but it is also a familiar feature of daily life. A handshake is a ritual which expresses greeting. Ritual may be simple like the handshake or complex like an involved ceremony. It involves the whole person at the physical, emotional and mental levels. It is a profound form of human expression. Ritual realizes, that is, makes real, what it expresses. It accomplishes this in and through the act of expression itself. The handshake not only expresses greeting, but in doing so it realizes the greeting, makes it to exist, to be. This is what is meant by the principle that sacraments effect what they signify: in the very act of expression, they realize what they express. Sacraments are realizing expression.

It follows from this that what a sacrament accomplishes and means is contained in its ritual expression. The ritual is the vehicle of its significance and efficacy. An understanding of a sacrament requires, therefore, knowledge and appreciation of its ritual.

Ritual is a public community activity and, as a particular genre of human activity, it follows laws of its own. Like all forms of life, it follows a law of growth in accordance with its own nature. A simple basic rite tends to expand from an inherent necessity to bring to expression its deeper meaning, and in doing so it tends to gather round it a cluster of minor rites, expressive of different aspects of its own loaded significance. Such development can easily result in an over-elaborate, florid ceremonial were it not that ritual also has an innate conservative character which, at least following a period of development, tends to resist change and to maintain its basic shape. The history of christian sacramental ritual exhibits both these characteristics of development and conservative tradition.

Since the primary source for an undersanding of a sacrament is its ritual, we turn now to a study of the ritual of the sacraments of christian initiation. This ritual has its own history and it can be understood only in the context and terms of this history. We engage here, then, on a survey of the ritual of baptism and confirmation as this has developed in the history of the Church. This, however, is no easy task. We are faced with a very complex story where there are still many gaps in our knowledge and where there are still many areas awaiting and requiring research. It is not simply that the basic ritual of initiation develops over the centuries, but it develops in different ways in different places. In particular, there is a significant difference in the history of the rite between East and West. It will not be possible to discuss in detail here this whole complex history. Instead, this study will concentrate on the basic liturgy of the Western Church, and especially on the Roman rite. It was the Roman rite which eventually prevailed throughout the West and which, from the Middle Ages to the Second Vatican Council, became, with but minor variations, the established rite of christian initiation in the Western Church. Discussion of the Eastern rite will here have to be confined to questions of comparison with this Western rite.

The third and fourth centuries are the classic period when this Roman rite was in full flower. Though there are still questions of detail which await an answer, sources for this period are abundant in the rich heritage of christian literature which has survived. The same, unfortunately, is not true of the earlier period, the first and second centuries, when the later developed rite was still in process of formation. Here we have to depend mainly on the evidence of the New Testament and incidental allusions in other early christian writings. For the most part, reference to the ritual of christian initiation throughout this period is tantalizingly inexplicit. Following the classic period of the third-fourth centuries, the history of the rite becomes the story of its adaptation to changing historical, geographical and social conditions. This period of adaptation extends into the later Middle Ages, when eventually the rite solidifies into a set mould which prevails until our own times and the reforms initiated by Vatican II.

Our survey is determined by this sequence of significant periods in the history of the ritual of christian initiation. I must emphasize again, however, that this survey can in no way claim to be a comprehensive discussion of this complex history. For this the reader is referred to the more specialized studies listed at the end of this work. Our interest here lies in the basic shape of the Western, and therefore the Roman, rite of christian initiation. The treatment must inevitably be a study in outline.

The Early Rite

We have already seen that christian initiation in the early Church consisted of two rites, baptism and imposition of hands. But we have also noted that the New Testament nowhere describes this ritual in any detail. What we get are allusions, pieces of incidental information. This information, however, does enable us to put together a general picture of the ritual of christian initiation in the early Church. We would expect that the earliest form of this ritual would have a comparatively simple character, but that as time went on a certain elaboration would occur. This is a law of liturgical life. The evidence fulfills this expectation.

In discussing the context of baptism in the life of the early Church, we saw that it belonged to the Church's missionary context, the context of evangelization, of preaching the gospel and the call to faith and conversion. It is difficult to imagine that the early Church ever considered this initial preaching sufficient preparation in christian faith and practice to warrant the immediate baptism of those who responded to this call. Some further instruction must have been required and the New Testament and other early sources give evidence of this.[1] That such instruction could in the

---

[1]On preparation for baptism in the New Testament period, see: Michel Dujarier, *A History of the Catechumenate: The First Six Centuries* (New York: Sadlier, 1979), 9-26; M. Martini, "Christian Initiation and Fundamental Theology: Reflections on the Stages of Christian Maturation in the Primitive Church," in *Problems and Perspectives of Fundamental Theology*, eds. R. Latourelle and G. O'Collins (New York: Paulist Press, 1982), 59-65.

very early period take a rudimentary form is indicated by a number of instances in Acts, for example, the Ethiopian eunuch (Chap. 8), the gaoler at Philippi and his household (Chap. 16), the twelve at Ephesus (Chap. 19). But one would expect that with time a more systematic approach would develop. This would be required especially in the case of pagan converts, who would need much more instruction than Jews in matters of christian belief and the christian way of life. The early christian document known as The Didaché, which in these matters probably provides evidence of first century christian practice, is helpful here in filling out the sparse evidence of the New Testament. This document is the first treatise of church or canon law and contains instructions on how to prepare candidates for baptism, on the way baptism should be performed and on the celebration of the eucharist. The preparation for baptism in this document consists of moral instruction based on a Jewish model which speaks of the Two Ways, the Way of Life (morally good conduct) and the Way of Death (morally bad conduct). Only when this instruction has been given and personally appropriated should one proceed to baptize the person. Eventually this primitive form of christian catechesis will evolve into the formal catechumenate of the later Church. Here also the emphasis will be on moral instruction and preparation.

However rudimentary may have been the preparation of converts for baptism in the early years of the Church's existence, it is clear that such preparation existed and formed an important aspect of the Church's missionary activity. With the expansion of the christian mission to embrace non-Jews throughout the Roman Empire, greater attention had to be paid to this instruction. The emphasis now had to fall on the moral training of the candidates to enable them to make the demanding transition from a pagan to a christian way of life. This emphasis would not have been required to anything like the same degree in the case of Jewish converts.

When the Church was satisfied that converts were ready for christian initiation, it admitted them to baptism. From the beginning the act of baptism consisted of immersion in running water, that is, in natural pools and streams. That this was the christian practice could be taken for granted because of the borrowing of the rite from Judaism. In any case, this is implied by the term itself: "to baptize" means "to dip in/under" water. St. Paul's reference in Romans 6:4 to being "buried" with Christ by baptism also implies immersion, since an allusion to the actual rite is required at this point of his argument. The description of the baptism of the Ethiopian eunuch in Acts would seem to be incompatible with any other form: "they both went down into the water, Philip and the eunuch, and he baptized him. And when they came up out of the water...." (Acts 8:38-39). Further information on the early practice is again provided by *The Didachē*. It states that baptism should be performed "in running water", that is, in streams or rivers. It then goes on:

> But if you have not running water, baptize in other water; and if you cannot in cold, then in warm. And if you have not either, pour forth water thrice upon the head.... (*Didachē* 7).[2]

It is clear from the reference here to "running water" that immersion is the normal form of baptism envisaged by this text. But the Church also accepts and practices a pouring of water on the head, baptism by infusion. This, however, is only allowed as an exception, when water for immersion is not available.

Earlier in this study we noted the primitive reference to calling on the name of Jesus at baptism and the evidence that this may have taken the form of an early credal, christological formula, such as "Jesus is Lord". The later trinitarian baptismal formula mentioned in Matthew 28:19 is very probably a development of this "calling on the name". *The Didachē* corroborates the evidence of Matthew on the use of this baptismal formula. It states that one should "baptize in

---

[2]Translation by E. C. Whitaker, *Documents of the Baptismal Liturgy*, (London: SPCK, 1970[2]), 1.

the Name of the Father and of the Son and of the Holy Spirit" (*Didachē* 7). This is probably a summary formula which refers to a rudimentary form of credal questions and responses, such as we find in a more developed form in the later baptismal ritual. Such responses would constitute the candidate's formal, public profession of christian faith which his baptism involved. The evidence would certainly seem to warrant the conclusion that well before the end of the first century the Church practiced a primitive form of credal questions and responses in the act of baptism.

The rite of imposition of hands for the reception of the Spirit followed baptism in the practice of the early Church and together with baptism constituted the full ceremony of christian initiation. This rite is mentioned or referred to in three passages of the New Testament, Acts 8:14-19; 19:6; Hebrews 6:2. We have already discussed the significance of the rite and its place in christian initiation. The gesture probably consisted of an outstretching of the hands in prayer and then a placing or leaning of them on the head of the person. The account of the episode in Samaria in Acts 8 suggests that this rite was reserved to recognised leaders in the Church, a suggestion certainly not contradicted but rather supported by Paul's action at Ephesus (Acts 19:1-7). This would also explain the reservation of this rite to the bishop in the later liturgy of initiation. But the missionary activity of Philip described in Acts 8 shows that, at least during the early missionary period, baptism itself could be performed by missionary preachers who did not have authority from the Church to complete the ceremony of initiation by the imposition of hands. The practice in this early period may have been rather fluid and one can understand how the Church at Jerusalem would wish to play a role in the expanding mission. But the action of Paul at Ephesus (Acts 19:1-7), where imposition of hands follows immediately on the baptism of the twelve, suggests that in normal practice the two rites went together and formed the complex unity of christian initiation. The role of the bishop at christian initiation in later periods reflects this practice and represents a systematization of it when structures of ecclesiastical authority had been more clearly defined.

Before concluding this discussion of the ritual of initiation in the early Church, a word needs to be said about the suggestion that this ritual included a rite of anointing after baptism. The main text appealed to in support of this suggestion is 2 Corinthians 1:21-22. Today, however, scripture scholars of all persuasions are convinced that the reference to anointing in this text is purely figurative. There is no evidence in the New Testament that christian initiation in this early period involved a rite of anointing. This rite, which subsequently became so prominent a feature of this ritual, was, therefore, a later development.[3]

The picture of christian initiation in the early Church which the evidence presents reveals a process which consists of the doctrinal and moral preparation of evangelized converts which culminates in the ceremony of baptism and imposition of hands, which constitutes their initiation as members of the Church. This was the foundation which the Church in subsequent centuries developed into its impressive process and ritual of christian initiation.[4]

The Classic Period

The liturgy of early Christianity, from what we can know of it from references in the New Testament and other early sources, has a simple and direct character. The early Church seems to have performed the essential rites with little elaboration. Apart from a famous passage in the writings of Justin Martyr around the middle of the second century, which is neither as detailed or explicit as one would wish, we

---

[3]On this question, see R. Schnackenburg, *Baptism in the Thought of St. Paul*, 89-91; also, I. de la Potterie, "Anointing of the Christian by Faith," in I. de la Potterie and S. Lyonnet, *The Christian Lives by the Spirit* (New York: Alba, 1971, trans. from French), 79-144.

[4]A readable discussion of the ritual of christian initiation in this early period may be found in A. Kavanagh, *The Shape of Baptism: The Rite of Christian Initiation* (New York: Pueblo Publishing Co., 1978), 11-30.

do not get clear evidence of the christian rites again until the beginning of the third century.[5] From then on, however, information is more abundant and we are able to form a fairly clear picture of how the Church celebrated its sacramental rites. The third and fourth centuries were the great period of christian liturgy. It was then the liturgy attained the peak of its development and its most impressive form. The earlier, simpler ritual now appears filled out and elaborated with various symbols, prayers and minor rites. An inherent necessity of liturgy was at work in this development. Ritual was here striving to achieve a greater breadth and depth of expressiveness. In achieving this, it attained also a more systematised, formal shape, the shape of a coherent, well-proportioned ceremony. Christian liturgy has here achieved that note of impressive solemnity essential to good ritual.

Throughout the Church at this period, in both East and West, the christian rites display the same, basic form. This basic identity, however, also shows up certain contrasts and variations which have developed, both between East and West and between the great centres, such as Rome, Alexandria, Antioch, and their satellite provinces. The provinces generally preserve and display a more archaic form of liturgy than the great centres. Thus, in the West from this period on, Rome presents a more developed liturgy than that of the surrounding provinces. With time, interaction will occur and a mutual influence will eventually issue in the Middle Ages in the standard liturgy of the Western Church.

This long and complicated liturgy cannot be treated here with any form of adequacy. This discussion will have to be a study in outline and therefore the concentration will fall on the Roman rite, the central and dominant rite of the West and that which shapes the western liturgical development.[6]

---

[5]Justin Martyr, *First Apology*, 61, 65.

[6]For further documentation and discussion of this topic, see E. C. Whitaker, *op. cit.*; T. Marsh, "The History and Significance of the Post-Baptismal Rites," *Irish Theological Quarterly*, 39(1962), 175-206.

We are fortunate to possess from the beginning of our period a document which describes the liturgy at Rome at that time. This is the *Apostolic Tradition* of Hippolytus, which most scholars agree in dating to around 215 A.D. This work gives a description of the Roman rite of christian initiation at this time and this gives us a sure starting-point for our period and a basis for identifying and assessing later developments. It provides the axis around which the later history of the rite revolves. We begin, then, by quoting this description of the Roman rite at the beginning of the third century.[7]

XX

7. Those who are to receive baptism shall fast on the Preparation (Friday) and on the Sabbath (Saturday). And on the Sabbath the bishop shall assemble those who are to be baptized in one place, and shall bid them all to pray and bow the knee.

8. And laying his hand on them he shall exorcise every evil spirit to flee away from them and never to return to them henceforward. And when he has finished exorcizing, let him breathe on their faces and seal their foreheads and ears and noses and then let him raise them up.

9. And they shall spend all the night in vigil, reading the scriptures to them and instructing them.

10. Moreover those who are to be baptized shall not bring any other vessel, save that which each will bring with him for the eucharist. For it is right for every one to bring his oblation then.

XXI

1. And at the hour when the cock crows they shall first (of all) pray over the water.

[7]Translation by Gregory Dix, *The Apostolic Tradition,* (London: SPCK, 1937).

2. When they come to the water, let the water be pure and flowing.

3. And they shall put off their clothes.

4. And they shall baptize the little children first. And if they can answer for themselves, let them answer. But if they cannot, let their parents answer or someone from their family.

5. And next they shall baptize the grown men; and last the women, who shall have loosed their hair and laid aside their gold ornaments. Let no one go down to the water having any alien object with them.

6. And at the time determined for baptizing, the bishop shall give thanks over the oil and put it into a vessel and it is called the Oil of Thanksgiving.

7. And he shall take other oil and exorcise over it, and it is called the Oil of Exorcism.

8. And let a deacon carry the Oil of Exorcism and stand on the left hand. And another deacon shall take the Oil of Thanksgiving and stand on the right hand.

9. And when the presbyter takes hold of each one of those who are to be baptized, let him bid him renounce saying:

   I renounce thee, Satan, and all thy service and all thy works.

10. And when he has said this let him anoint with the Oil of Exorcism, saying:

   Let all evil spirits depart far from thee.

11. Then after these things let him give over to the presbyter who stands at the water. And let them stand in the water naked. And let a deacon likewise go down with him into the water.

12. And he goes down to the water; let him who baptizes lay hand on him saying thus:

Dost thou believe in God the Father Almighty?

13. And he who is being baptized shall say:

I believe.

14. Let him forthwith baptize (dip) him once, having his hand laid upon his head.

15. And after (this) let him say:

Dost thou believe in Christ Jesus, the Son of God,
Who was born of Holy Spirit and the Virgin Mary,
Who was crucified in the days of Pontius Pilate,
And died,
And rose the third day living from the dead
And ascended into the heavens,
And sat down at the right hand of the Father,
And will come to judge the living and the dead?

16. And when he says: I believe, let him baptize him the second time.

17. And again let him say:

Dost thou believe in the Holy Spirit in the Holy Church, And the resurrection of the flesh?

18. And he who is being baptized shall say: I believe. And so let him baptize him the third time.

19. And afterwards when he comes up he shall be anointed with the Oil of Thanksgiving saying:

I anoint thee with holy oil in the Name of Jesus Christ.

20. And so each one drying himself they shall now put on their clothes, and after this let them be together in the assembly.

XXII

1. And the bishop shall lay his hand upon them invoking and saying:

   O Lord God, who didst count these worthy of deserving the forgiveness of sins by the laver of regeneration, make them worthy to be filled with thy Holy Spirit and send upon them thy grace, that they may serve thee according to thy will; to thee is the glory, to the Father and to the Son with the Holy Ghost in the holy Church, both now and ever and world without end. Amen.

2. After this pouring the consecrated oil and laying his hand on his head, he shall say:

   I anoint thee with holy oil in God the Father Almighty and Christ Jesus and the Holy Ghost.

3. And sealing him on the forehead, he shall give him the kiss of peace and say:

   The Lord be with you.
   And he who has been sealed shall say:
   And with thy spirit.

4. And so shall he do to each one severally.

5. Thenceforward they shall pray together with all the people. But they shall not previously pray with the faithful before they have undergone these things.

   And after the prayers, let them give the kiss of peace.

   (A description of the celebration of the eucharist then follows).

The ceremony of christian initiation described here takes place at the Easter Vigil on the night of Holy Saturday. The climax of the ceremony is the celebration of the eucharist at dawn on Easter Sunday. This was the first time the newly baptized participated in the complete eucharist and received communion. This choice of time for christian initiation was totally deliberate and expresses the significance of the event as bringing about union with Christ and participation in the paschal mystery of his death and resurrection. The culmination of initiation in the celebration of the eucharist shows an awareness of the eucharist as the central act of the Church's being and existence. The Church is the eucharistic community and to become a member of the Church means participating in this, its central action. Initiation into the Church thus logically means initiation to the eucharist. One cannot fail to notice in Hippolytus' description of the ceremony that the comparatively simple rite of the earlier period has here been elaborated into a formal and stately ceremony. Liturgy's inherent tendency to achieve adequate ceremonial expression has clearly been at work, and with considerable success, during the second century.

The first observation that has to be made on the ceremony as presented here is that it consists of three parts: the pre-baptismal ceremonies (XX, 7-XXI,10); baptism and its attendant ceremonies (XXI, 11-20); the post-baptismal rites and conclusion (XXII, 1-6). These three parts form together one integral unity, a whole, the rite of christian initiation. Yet, each also constitutes a unit in itself and has its own independent significance. We will discuss each of these parts separately, following the order and rhythm of the ceremony as it moves forward to its final conclusion.

The Catechumenate

The ceremonies before the baptism constitute the conclusion of the candidates' preparation for initiation. We have noted already the evidence from the earlier period for the existence and form of this preparation. Here we see that by the beginning of the third century this already developed into the classical catechumenate. The catechumenate, as it developed, consisted of both a remote and an immediate preparation for baptism. When a person decided they would like to become a Christian, they were formally enrolled among the catechumens, that is, those under instruction for baptism. The preparation which then began was no hurried affair. It could last up to three years, or even longer. It consisted of instruction, mainly of a moral kind, formation in christian attitudes, prayer, blessings, exorcisms. When the catechumen was adjudged to have made sufficient progress in this formation, he could be formally enrolled at the beginning of Lent among those to be baptized the following Easter. The immediate preparation of the candidate for baptism now began, extending over the whole period of Lent until the actual baptism at the Easter Vigil.

Throughout these weeks of Lent this group, called The Chosen (*Electi*), underwent a more intensive programme of doctrinal and moral instruction and sacramental and spiritual preparation. This sacramental or ritual element consisted of ceremonies called Scrutinies. The term comes from the Latin verb *scrutare*, which means "to penetrate", and the ceremony was called *scrutinium* because its purpose was to allow the transforming power of God to penetrate the catechumen, remove him from the dominion of Satan and effectively prepare him for discipleship of Christ through baptism. The essential rite was an exorcism consisting of imposition of hands and a prayer asking God to destroy Satan's hold over the person. Eventually, three such scrutinies took place at Mass on three Sundays of Lent, the third, fourth and fifth Sundays. The theme of the Mass on these occasions, in the prayers, the biblical readings and the homily, was baptism. The catechumens attended only this liturgy of the word; they were dismissed before the eucharist proper began.

At a late stage in the process, eventually on the fifth Sunday of Lent, the catechumens were taught the Creed, the form known to us as the Apostles' Creed which is really the baptismal Creed of the ancient Church. The Creed was a summary of the teaching of the Gospels, a summary of the christian faith. The doctrinal instruction given to the candidates during Lent concentrated on giving them a basic understanding of the Creed's meaning.

This Lenten catechumenal process concluded with a special ceremony on Holy Saturday. In Hippolytus this ceremony takes place at the Vigil immediately before the baptism, but later it was transferred to the morning, thus separating the ceremonies of the catechumenate from those of christian initiation proper. In this rite the candidates were asked to recite the Creed and the Lord's Prayer, which they had first been taught some weeks previously, the "giving back" (*redditio*), as it was called, of these texts. This was followed by an exorcism which included the Epheta Rite, that is, the touching of the ears of the candidate with saliva in imitation of the gesture of Jesus in Mark 7:31-35. The Church saw a baptismal implication and application in this incident: the opening of the ears represented the gift of faith, the hearing and acceptance of the gospel. There followed the solemn rite of the renunciation of Satan and his works and pomps. This rite was a fitting climax to the long and arduous catechumenate, since the whole thrust of the process was towards weaning the catechumen from the allegiances of his former life, represented by the figure of Satan, and training him in the ways of christian living. We find here the basic concept and emphasis of the catechumenate, that transition from one way of life to another which St. Paul described in terms of the two ages of salvation history.

Attached to the rite of renunciation was a final exorcism, involving here an anointing of the candidate. Though originally this was an extensive corporal anointing, it was eventually curtailed to consist simply of an anointing between the shoulder blades and on the breast. As with all the pre-baptismal exorcisms, this rite also was a prayer for the catechumen's transformation by the grace of God. The anointing with oil symbolized the strengthening power of this grace for the combat of the christian life.

As with all liturgical processes, the catechumenate also developed over the centuries. The trend was towards a greater formalization and rigidity of the whole process and its ceremonies. But the basic concept remained intact. The catechumenate was meant to be a thorough and realistic training of the candidate for baptism, preparing him or her for the radical transformation of life which the transition from paganism and its associations to christianity involved.[8]

The Baptism

With the completion of the catechumenal rites, the candidates were now ready for their baptism.[9] The baptismal service on the Saturday night began with the blessing of the water for baptism and the oil for the anointing after baptism. The blessing of the water became a major feature of the service. It involved a number of lengthy prayers and gestures of blessing. These prayers contain a full exposition of the meaning of baptism and would form a study on their own. This ceremony, however, was not a primitive feature of the ritual of baptism. It was a development and marks a change from the old practice of baptizing in the open air in running water to baptizing indoors in a specially constructed pool. This change occurred probably in the course of the second century and was probably dictated by practical considerations, such as convenience, numbers, climate. It was when this move indoors began that it was felt necessary to have a special ceremony for the blessing of the water. When the water and oil had been blessed, the baptism of the candidates took place. For reasons of modesty, since the candidates had to be practically naked, baptism and the anointing after it took place in privacy, with only the necessary ministers present. Each one individually stood in the water, the minister placed his hand on the head and asked the triple questions of the Creed:

[8]On the catechumenate in the ancient Church, see M. Dujarier, *op. cit.*; R. Beraudy, "Les Rites Prebaptismaux," in *L'Eglise en Priere: Introduction a la Liturgie*, ed. A. G. Martimort (Paris, Desclee, 1965³), 543-551.

[9]On the rite of baptism in the ancient Church, see R. Beraudy, "Le Bapteme et ses preparations," *loc. cit.*, 529-566; E. Yarnold, *The Awe-Inspiring Rites of Christian Initiation: Baptismal Homilies of the Fourth Century* (London: St. Paul Publications, 1971); A. Kavanagh, *op. cit.*, 35-63.

Do you believe in God, the Father Almighty ....?
Do you believe in Jesus Christ ....?
Do you believe in the Holy Spirit ....?

To each question the candidate answered "I do believe" and each time the minister dipped him under the water. No formula other than these credal questions and responses accompanied the act of baptism.

When the newly baptized came out of the water, they were anointed with oil. Hippolytus calls this oil Oil of Thanksgiving but later witnesses describe it as Chrism. This post-baptismal anointing is well attested throughout the West from this period on, but, as we shall see, there is a serious question about its existence in the East. At the time of Hippolytus this rite comprised an extensive anointing of the body — it took place before the baptized resumed their clothes. This must have added significantly to the length of the whole ceremony and later we find it reduced to an anointing of the crown of the head.

The main question which arises concerning this rite is the question of its origin and meaning. We have already seen that there was no rite of anointing in the ritual of baptism in the period of the New Testament. The rite, therefore, was a later development, introduced sometime in the course of the second century. Why was it introduced? What was its significance? Fortunately, there is evidence available which enables us to give at least a general answer to these intriguing questions.

First, it is worth noting that in ancient times, when people took a bath, they rubbed oil on their bodies, anointed themselves, before and after the washing. Before the bath the oil served as a soap and after it it functioned as a perfume. This secular use of anointing associated with washing provides the background which must have suggested the idea of anointing after baptism. But what religious significance was attached to the rite? We find an indication of this in the reference of St. Paul in 2 Corinthians 2:14-15, where he describes Christians as the fragrance and aroma of Christ. In the ancient Church this text is often applied to the newly baptized and the event of baptism. We have to remember here that the term Christ means in Greek, as Messiah in Hebrew, "the Anointed One". The earliest references to the post-baptismal anointing associate it with the baptized person's assumption of the name of Christ: he or she is now a Christian. The formula accompanying the rite in the *Apostolic Tradition* speaks of the Name of Christ: "I anoint thee with holy oil in the Name of Jesus Christ". In origin the rite expressed the assumption of Christ's name. We noted earlier in this study the strong meaning which a a name had in Judaism and early Christianity: it stood for that whose name it was. To be anointed in the Name of Christ is thus similar in meaning to being baptized in his name. It means consecration to the service of Christ, belonging to him, taking his name, discipleship. Soon another implication of belonging to Christ and assuming his name was associated with the rite. The anointing was performed by pouring oil on the head and letting it run down over the body. This action recalled the reference in Psalm 133:2, to the anointing of Aaron, his consecration as High Priest and source of the priesthood of the Old Testament (cf. Exodus 30:23-33): "It is like the precious oil upon the head, running down upon the beard, upon the beard of Aaron. . . " The physical resemblance between this anointing of Aaron and the anointing after baptism seems to have suggested an interpretation of this latter in terms of participation in the priesthood of Christ. The priesthood of Aaron was an Old Testament figure or type fulfilled in Christ, the true, eternal King and Priest. The post-baptismal anointing brought this association to mind and thus came to be seen as expressing the Christian's participation in the royal priesthood of Christ mentioned in 1 Peter 2:9. This significance of the rite, as also that of the assumption of Christ's name, has remained constant in later tradition. The rite was also eventually seen as expessing participation in Christ's anointing with the Spirit referred to in Luke 4:18 and Acts 10:38. Here again we are dealing with an aspect of belonging to Christ, an implication of discipleship.[10]

All these interpretations of the post-baptismal anointing bring out different aspects of the meaning of baptism. It was a baptismal rite, an attendant ceremony of baptism emphasizing different aspects of the significance of the sacrament. The very situation of the rite, immediately after the baptism before the person had even resumed their clothes, shows this. It pointed back to the act of baptism just concluded and forward to the new life to which the Christian was now committed, the living out of the life of discipleship.

A later feature of the baptismal ritual which does not appear in Hippolytus is the clothing of the newly baptized in a white robe. This was a later introduction and took place after the anointing. The white robe symbolized the new status of the Christian and was a simple and direct way of indicating the transition which baptism effected from the old existence to the new.

The Rite of the Spirit

Hippolytus has divided his description of christian initiation into two sections, the first, Section XXI of the *Apostolic Tradition*, devoted to the baptism and its attendant ceremonies (including here the concluding rites of the catechumenate) and the second, Section XXII, devoted to the rite for the giving of the Spirit performed by the bishop alone. These two sets of ceremonies were performed in different places, the baptismal ceremonies in the privacy of the baptistry, the rite of the Spirit in the midst of the congregation gathered in the church for the Easter Mass. Hippolytus marks this transition from the first phase of christian initiation to the second in his concluding remark on the baptismal rites.

---

[10]On the baptismal anointing, see L. L. Mitchell, *Baptismal Anointing* (London: SPCK, 1966); T. Marsh, "A Study of Confirmation II," *Irish Theological Quarterly* 39(1972), 319-336.

> And so each one drying himself (after the anointing) they shall now put on their clothes, and after this let them be together in the assembly (xxi,20).

The rite for the giving of the Spirit now takes place. The actions which Hippolytus describes, all performed by the bishop, consist of imposition of hand and an accompanying prayer and an anointing of the forehead in the form of a cross (sealing). The imposition of hand which accompanies the prayer, the first action mentioned, should be understood as an outstretching of the hands by the bishop, the traditional gesture of prayer and blessing. The text of the prayer leaves no doubt about the meaning of this gesture. The candidates are described as those counted "worthy of deserving the forgiveness of sins by the laver of regeneration", that is, as people already baptized. The prayer goes on to ask the Lord God to make these "worthy to be filled with thy Holy Spirit". The bishop then proceeds to lay his hand on the head of each one individually and anoints their forehead. Though the anointing mentioned here is, as we shall see, unusual, it is clear that the imposition of hand involved represents the application to each individual of the initial general imposition and prayer and the fulfilment of that gesture and prayer, that is, the giving of the Spirit by God. The meaning of this ceremony is quite plain: those already baptized are now through this rite filled with the Holy Spirit.

This Roman ritual of christian initiation at the beginning of the third century shows a striking similarity to that found in Acts, Chapters 8 and 19. This cannot be accidental and this Roman rite has to be regarded as a direct descendant of the ritual of initiation practiced by the early Church. We meet here again the same two basic references attached to the same rites, the christological reference of baptism and the pneumatological reference of the imposition of hands. There is little indication in the text of Hippolytus of any serious influence of Pauline thought. The *Apostolic Tradition* is a witness that the early Church's understanding and practice of christian initiation, as revealed in the Acts of the Apostles, has maintained itself into the third century.

The anointing which forms part of the imposition of hand in this Roman rite has been the subject of much discussion. It does not feature in the initiation liturgy of the western provinces, North Africa, Spain, North Italy, Gaul, in the third and fourth centuries. Throughout this period these areas practiced a sequence of initiation rites which consisted of baptism, the post-baptismal anointing and the imposition of hand. The same basic pattern is thus common to Rome and its provinces, with the exception of this signing of the forehead with oil by the bishop in the course of the imposition of hand at Rome. One must presume that originally Rome and these provinces practiced the same basic initiation ritual. If so, this unusual feature was a purely Roman development. There is some evidence that the post-baptismal anointing concluded with the making of the sign of the cross on the forehead, probably by the bishop. The reason for the Roman practice may lie here. At this period the number of candidates for baptism must have been substantially larger at Rome than in the remoter areas. It is easy to imagine that in these circumstances it would prove very inconvenient for the bishop, and for the smooth running of the ceremony, if he was personally involved in the anointing of each candidate after baptism. Yet, it would be felt desirable to maintain the act and role of the bishop here. An obvious solution to this practical, and in no way doctrinal, problem would be to combine this signing of the forehead with oil with the individual imposition of hand after the prayer for the Spirit, that is, in effect, to perform this imposition by way of signing the forehead with oil. It must have been in some such way that this feature of the Roman rite came to be.

The important conclusion which emerges from this discussion of the origin of this anointing in the Roman rite is that originally it was a feature of the post-baptismal anointing and formed no part of the rite of imposition of hand, but at some stage at Rome, for practical reasons, it was incorporated into this latter to become there, with the kiss of peace, the concluding act of the initiation ritual. Great trees grow from small seeds. This insignificant-looking act of anointing is destined to have a history out of all proportion to its origin.[11]

The rite of initiation concluded with this act of anointing. Hippolytus mentions in a general way prayers which followed and then proceeds to describe the celebration of the eucharist which now took place. This Roman rite of christian initiation developed in a number of minor ways over the following two centuries. The thrust of these developments was towards achieving a smoother and more economical ceremony. But the basic shape of the rite remained the same. It is easy to recognise in this rite the same essential form and sequence of actions that one finds in the references to initiation in the New Testament period. But there has also been development and a certain elaboration. Preparation for baptism has developed into the formal, structured catechumenate. Some minor rites have been added, especially the post-baptismal anointing and, at Rome, the incorporation of an anointing into the rite of imposition of hand. These rites, far from obscuring, are meant to highlight the two central rites of baptism and imposition of hand and to enhance the expressiveness of the whole ritual. The significance of christian initiation here is the same as in the New Testament. The essential reference of baptism is christological: it effects discipleship of Christ; the essential reference of the episcopal imposition of hand is pneumatological: it confers the gift of the Spirit. Together these two rites form a unity, one impressive ceremony, the rite of christian initiation. They make one a Christian, a member of the Church of Christ. The first act of the new Christian is to join with the community in the central action of christian worship, the celebration of the eucharist.

The Eastern Rite

No document comparable to the *Apostolic Tradition* has survived from the Eastern Church at this early date. It is

---

[11]For a general discussion of the history of the post-baptismal rites in the West, see T. Marsh, "The History and Significance of the Post-Baptismal Rites," *loc. cit.*

only from later in the third century that we begin to get some information about christian liturgy in the East. Though the same basic pattern is discernible, a significant difference now emerges here between the rite of initiation in the East and the West. The evidence in question concerns especially the great christian centre of Antioch which, leaving aside Alexandria in Egypt, inherited from Jerusalem the leadership of the Christian Church in the East. The striking difference is that the eastern or Antiochene rite does not appear to have had any rite after baptism, that is, there is no evidence of a post-baptismal anointing or a rite of imposition of hand for the giving of the Spirit. The giving of the Spirit, in fact, seems rather to be associated with the pre-baptismal anointing or even the laying of the hand on the head which is involved in the act of baptizing. This absence of a post-baptismal rite has occasioned much scholarly discussion. A view which has received some support maintains that this form of initiation represents an original christian practice which was at least an alternative, legitimate form to that found in Acts of the Apostles and the western liturgy. For a number of reasons, however, this view must be rejected.

As we saw in our study of the New Testament references, there is no evidence there that this form of initiation was an original, primitive practice. Moreover, evidence of this eastern liturgy is only available from about the middle of the third century. Prior to that date we have little definite information on the liturgy of the East. But throughout this period the Church in the East underwent a different experience to that in the West. There were more splinter groups there than in the West and it was just at this time that the Eastern Church in particular had to face and overcome the serious threat of Gnosticism in its various forms. What effect this turbulent situation may have had on liturgy is not easy to determine, given the lack of evidence. But pieces of evidence do exist which suggest, at least, that a change did occur at this time in the region where Antioch was the centre of influence. There is the evidence of Acts, the initiation liturgy with which Luke is familiar, consisting of baptism and imposition of hands. Since Luke must be placed in the region of Antioch's influence and leadership, very probably indeed in Antioch itself, it cannot credibly be maintained that this area did not once possess the post-baptismal rite for the gift of the Spirit. Further, one of the few studies which discusses this question and the texts concerned with thoroughness, *La Confirmation* by Lous Ligier (p. 95 ff.), has shown that these texts retain a reference to a post-baptismal imposition of hand for the gift of the Spirit which did not survive as an actual rite.[12] Other pieces of evidence, which we cannot rehearse here, support this view. The overall evidence suggests, therefore, that the East at some early stage discontinued the imposition of hands as a distinct rite. Why this occurred is not easy to determine, but there is some evidence that the change was associated with the eastern understanding of the role of the Spirit and its experience of conflicts in the Church concerned with this role. It has to be remembered, too, that the mentality of the East at this stage still had a pronounced biblical, semitic character. This involved a different way of understanding time and sacrament to that operative in the West. This, too, may have been a factor in the development. But while discontinuing the distinct rite of the Spirit, the East did preserve the pneumatological reference of christian initiation. It is unlikely ,however, that the association of the pre-baptismal anointing with the Spirit, unknown in the West, should be seen as part of this reference. The role of the Spirit envisaged here is not the eschatological gift which initiation involves, but rather the New Testament theme of the role of the Spirit in conversion and the gift of faith. Rather, with the discontinuance of the special rite of the Spirit in this liturgy, the gift of the Spirit was seen as involved in baptism itself.

Later again, however, beginning apparently in the latter part of the fourth century, the East gradually restored a post-baptismal rite, an anointing of the forehead, and attached to it the pneumatological reference of christian initia-

[12]L. Ligier, *La Confirmation: Sens et Conjoncture Oecumenique Hier et Aujourd'hui* (Paris: Beauchesne, 1973).

...ove seems to have been associated with the
...ssertion, against the so-called Macedonian
...he divinity of the Spirit, a doctrine defined at the
...Constantinople in 381. The introduction of this
...origin of the Byzantine rite of christian initiation
prac... by the Greek Orthodox Church, which consists of
baptism and this post-baptismal anointing for the gift of the
Spirit.

Adaptation and Disintegration

The liturgy of christian initiation reached the peak of its
development in the third and fourth centuries. It was then
that it struck that delicate balance between understatement
and overstatement, between the freshness of originality and
the conservatism of tradition which is the hall-mark of
maturity at its peak and the definition of the classic. Here,
christian experience and christian ritual most closely coin-
cide; the ritual was truly a disclosive expression of the
experience it sought to encapsulate.

Before the fourth century had ended, however, signs had
already appeared that this happy situation was not going to
last.

The Peace of Constantine (313), and the patronage of the
Emperor which accompanied it, faced the Christian Church
with a new, and in some ways disconcerting, situation. If
there were advantages for the Church in this new situation,
there were also some less obvious disadvantages which only
time would reveal. Christianity had suddenly become
respectable; to be a Christian could now be socially advan-
tageous. It is hardly surprising that in this changed climate
the number of christian converts rapidly increased. Nor is it
surprising that the Church now became less vigilant in its
admission of candidates to baptism. The new situation put a
strain on the old catechumenate which had been developed
to meet the different needs of a different period. There is
evidence that already in the course of the fourth century a
certain air of complacency began to develop here and that

the rigour of the old system was significantly relaxed. Two inevitable developments now followed which seriously affected the practice of christian initiation which the Church had developed over the preceding centuries.[13]

The first of these developments was dictated by the increased membership of the Church. Christian communities now existed in every town throughout the Empire, and even throughout the courtyside. The old concept of the christian community gathered round its chief priest, the bishop, in his city church was no longer adequate here. These communities required their own services celebrated by their own ministers in their own local churches. This applied also to christian initiation and gradually the practice developed of allowing priests in these local churches to administer the catechumenate and baptism. The Church in the West, however, attempted to maintain the old concept of the unified rite of initation by reserving to the bishop the post-baptismal episcopal rite of imposition of hand and chrismation. As the bishop could only perform this role by visiting, if and when he could, these outlying churches of his diocese and administering this rite to those baptized sometime previously, the one ceremony of christian initiation now came to be divided into two, baptism and the episcopal rite of the Spirit, or confirmation, as it now came to be called from the fifth century on. This procedure, however, was not totally new. It had long been traditional practice in the case of catechumens who were seriously ill. These would be baptized by priests privately, on their sick bed — hence the name clinical baptism — and then later, if they recovered, would receive the post-baptismal rite from the bishop. What now happened was that this exceptional practice gradually became general in the West, though the old practice of the one unified ceremony of initiation continued in the bishop's own church at Easter and Pentecost and for many centuries yet continued to be regarded as the norm. In the East the same problem presented itself, but there a

[13]On the history of christian initiation after the classical period, see J. D. C. Fisher, *Christian Initiation: Baptism in the Medieval West* (London: SPCK, 1965).

different solution was adopted. Priests were here allowed to perform the post-baptismal anointing immediately after baptism. The integrity of the rite of initiation was in this way maintained, but at the expense of the presence of the bishop.

The second development which, from the fifth century on, significantly influenced the shape and understanding of the rite of initiation was that the majority, and eventually the totality, of candidates for baptism were now infants. Though infants and children were always considered as proper candidates for baptism, and are explicitly mentioned by Hippolytus, the rite itself envisaged adult candidates and was devised purely for such. The whole ritual, actions and verbal statements, were addressed to adults and required their responses. The realism of the rite and the efficacy of its expression depended on this. The change in the candidates for initiation from adults to infants was not an abrupt one. It came about gradually over a long period of time, in fact, a few centuries. Perhaps because of this very gradualness of the change, no major alteration of the rite was undertaken to adjust it to the new situation. Though some more obvious, though minor, anomalies were removed or softened, the rite continued to address the infant as if it were an adult and some realism was salvaged by having the sponsors make the responses. But in the new situation with which the Church was confronted from the fifth century on, that situation which over a few centuries gave birth to the Middle Ages, the Church was forced to adapt its old system of christian initiation to meet the new circumstances which now came to prevail. Some significant consequences of this adaptation must now be mentioned.

The fact that the candidates for baptism were now almost exclusively infants automatically meant the disappearance of the old catechumenate, except in missionary situations. The ceremonies of the catechumenate, however, were continued and administered to the infants, but now they were telescoped together to form the opening ceremonies of the baptismal rite. For a long time baptism was conferred in local churches only at the traditional seasons, Easter and Pentecost. This ensured that the sacrament's communal and ecclesial character continued to be properly asserted. But as Augustine's doctrine of original sin gained ground, with its insistence that infants who died without baptism could not enter the Kingdom of Heaven, this ancient practice was changed. The Church now came to insist that infants be baptized as quickly as possible after birth. Baptism was now understood mainly as the means of wiping out original sin. In meaning and celebration it was now a private, very individualistic rite, celebrated at any time that was convenient and involving only the infant, the priest and a few relations. The communal, ecclesial emphasis so central to the old form was here almost entirely lost.

The reservation of confirmation, the completion of initiation, to the bishop, understandable in its origin as adherence to old tradition and as a way of maintaining some concept of the unity of christian initiation, now from the fifth centry on began to cause great practical problems. The admirable theory was that the bishop would visit regularly his outlying churches and confirm those who had been baptized in the meantime. But the disturbed condition of Europe in the period between 500 A.D. and 800 A.D., the breakdown of the system of communications, the great size of continental dioceses, all these factors ensured that the implementation of this theory was practically impossible. Moreover, the bishop now had become a prominent political figure in addition to being an ecclesiastic and much of his time was devoted to political affairs. Sees, also, could be left vacant for a considerable number of years. In these circumstances the discrepancy between theory and practice became very wide indeed. In fact, for the period mentioned, in many of the western provinces, and apart from the papal See of Rome itself which stubbornly adhered to the old tradition, the theory just ceased to operate. For much of this period these areas, including even the episcopal churches, ceased to perform the episcopal rite of imposition of hand and chrismation and concluded initiation with the anointing immediately following the baptism. This now was regarded in these regions as constituting full initiation and it had the great advantage that the complete rite could now be administered by the priest on the one occasion in his own church without any awkward requirement of awaiting a problematic visit by the bishop. The sources here do not inform us how this rather radical break with western and Roman liturgical tradition actually came about or how it was understood or justified. They simply present us with the fact. But it is easy enough to identify at least some of the factors which probably suggested and led to this development. The unsettled conditions of the time, which we have mentioned, was one such. A further implication of this was that Rome's communication with the provinces had now become somewhat tenuous and it was no longer therefore in a position to check wayward developments in these faraway areas, or perhaps even to realize what was happening. Again, the post-baptismal anointing, which here attained a new prominence, was now seen, in addition to its older significances, as expressing the Christian's anointing with the Spirit, an interpretation which, though basically baptismal in meaning, could easily enough be stretched to embrace the reference to the gift of the Spirit essential to christian initiation. Finally, the similarity between this form of initiation and that of the Eastern Church cannot be totally a coincidence. The links between the East and areas such as North Italy and Southern Gaul at this period were particularly strong and the suitability of the eastern initiation rite to meet the needs of the churches in these areas must also have been an influential factor.

The restoration of the Roman form of christian initiation was the work of Charlemagne, or rather of his minister, Alcuin of York, at the end of the eighth and beginning of the ninth centuries.[14] Charlemagne obtained texts from Rome of the Roman celebration of sacraments and diffused copies of these throughout his vast territory, insisting that this model be followed in all the Churches of the Empire. In this way the episcopal rite of confirmation, that is, the post-baptismal imposition of hand and chrismation, was re-

---

[14]A readable account of this Carolingian liturgical reform may be found in G. Ellard *Master Alcuin, Liturgist* (Chicago, 1956).

stored to the rite of christian initiation in the West. The result, however, was not simply a return to the rite of Hippolytus and the classical period. For the Carolingian practice in episcopal churches was to administer baptism at the Easter Vigil and then on the following Sunday to confirm those baptized a week earlier. Those baptized in other churches now again had to await the visit of the bishop to receive confirmation. Thus, the separation of baptism and confirmation which had begun in the latter part of the fourth century as a practical necessity here becomes a regular practice and attains the status of a norm.

The interval between baptism and confirmation, which had now become normative, lengthened with the passage of time. At first the old tradition was still sufficiently alive to require an insistence that confirmation be received as early as possible after baptism. Outside the cathedral city this would still mean an interval of some years, perhaps up to five. But when in later centuries the concept of "the age of discretion" developed, this came to be regarded as the appropriate time to receive confirmation. For a time there was considerable variation in deciding when this age occurred and practice fluctuated between seven years and twelve. Eventually, seven years came to be regarded as marking the time of discretion and by the end of the Middle Ages this had become the age for confirmation, with the exception of Spain which tended to retain the older practice of confirming between three and five.

We noted earlier in this study that christian initiation, being initiation into the Church, meant initiation into the Church's central action, the celebration of the eucharist. In the old classic rite celebrated at Easter and Pentecost, the celebration of the eucharist was the climax towards which the whole ceremony moved. Participation in the eucharist and reception of communion here formed the culmination of christian initiation. With the separation of baptism and confirmation a question now arose concerning first communion, particularly since the candidates in question were infants or young children. For a long time the practice here was to communicate infants after baptism, and therefore long before their confirmation. Until the Middle Ages infant first communion was the universal practice of the Church: The relation of baptism and the eucharist and the old sense of christian initiation as initiation to the eucharist was maintained in this practice. Then, during the early Middle Ages a new reverence developed towards the eucharistic elements involving a corresponding anxiety to protect them from accidents. Infants now were communicated with consecrated wine only, often by some form of intinction. But when, around the beginning of the thirteenth century, communion under one species began to become the general practice and the laity received the host only, the communion of infants ceased altogether. It was now held that children should not receive the eucharist until they were old enough to understand the meaning of the sacrament. First communion also now was postponed until the age of discretion and was received sometime after confirmation. By the time of the Council of Trent in the sixteenth century, with but a few exceptions, this practice had become standard throughout the Church.

The only subsequent change in the sequence of these sacraments has been a recent one. In the middle of the nineteenth century a custom developed in France of postponing confirmation until the age of twelve *after* first communion. The reason behind this move was to ensure that the child was well instructed in the catechism and the change brought with it the notion that knowledge of the catechism somehow pertained to confirmation. In the second half of the century this French custom came to be adopted by most other countries, again with the exception of Spain which long continued to maintain its older tradition. Though Rome disapproved of the change and over a long period of time sought to oppose it, it found itself helpless in the face of its popularity. Later again, at the beginning of this century, when Pope Pius X decreed that children be admitted to first communion at the age of seven, this earlier age now became the age for first communion. Thus came about the current practice in the Church which now again presents a sequence of baptism, first communion, confirmation. Roman approval for this sequence was finally given, implicitly at least, in the new Rite of Confirmation issued in 1971, which allows episcopal conferences to approve an age later than seven for conferring confirmation.

The rite of christian initiation of the classic period went through many vicissitudes and received many alterations in the centuries following the fourth. No grand concept dictated and determined these changes. They were mostly adaptations which began as *ad hoc* practical decisions in the changed circumstances and new pastoral situations which confronted the Church over these centuries. Eventually, the old concept of the one rite of initiation, incorporating baptism, confirmation and the eucharist, was dismantled to be replaced by an arrangement whereby these sacraments were conferred separately, and in a varying sequence, over a number of years. Commenting on this final result, J.D.C. Fisher aptly writes: "baptism, confirmation and first communion are now three events separated from one another in time, so much so that it has become difficult ever since to appreciate the organic unity of the undivided rite of initiation as we find it in the third and fourth centuries."[15] Circumstances forced adaptation and a practical pastoral concern was operating in the adaptations which occurred. Yet, whatever success in pastoral terms may have attended these developments, they also involved a disintegration of the unified rite of initiation and a corresponding weakening of the sense of coherence, solemnity and expressiveness which marked that rite. More serious, perhaps, is the fact that in dismantling this rite the new process did not replace the old concept with any coherent concept of its own. The new arrangement required a new understanding of initiation derived from, and not imposed upon, the new situation which this arrangement was devised to meet. This new understanding did not emerge. The whole history of the process of adaptation thus leaves one with a feeling of haphazard change, a sense of adaptation in search of a concept.

[15]J. D. C. Fisher, *op. cit.*, 139.

Chapter Seven

THEOLOGY AND DOCTRINE

The old principle *lex orandi, lex credendi* states that questions concerning the meaning of faith arise from the prayerful practice of faith. The sacraments are a good illustration of this principle. From time to time sacramental practice raised questions which could only be answered at the doctrinal level. These questions generally arose as disputed practical issues which then became doctrinal disputes. The Church's doctrine on baptism, for the most part, has its origin in these disputes. Confirmation, on the other hand, escaped controversy and the body of doctrine concerning it is much smaller. For many centuries confirmation continued to be a living practicve rather than a rite one speculated or disputed about. Eventually, its separation from baptism forced the question of its significance to theological attention. This chapter will be concerned with the theology and doctrine on these sacraments which have developed over the centuries.

The Doctrine of Baptism

What became the Church's accepted doctrine on baptism had its origin in doctrinal disputes concerning the sacrament in the ancient Church.[1] Eventually , the accepted positions which emerged from these disputes were organized by the scholastic theologians of the Middle Ages into a doctrinal system representing the Church's teaching on baptism. The writings which initiated baptismal doctrine were thus controversial and polemical in character. Meanwhile, the Church's baptismal instruction, both the catechumenal and especially the mystagogical, that is, the catechesis given in the weeks following the reception of baptism, show us a different kind of teaching. This is a pastoral instruction aimed at formation and spiritual edification. It preaches the meaning of baptism as we have seen this presented in the New Testament and in the liturgy. It is biblical in character using accepted baptismal themes of the Old and New Testament to communicate its message. It approaches baptism from a salvation history perspective rather than in a strictly theological way. Its basic theme is that of redemption in Christ which one achieves through union with Christ in baptism. The great preachers of the fourth and fifth centuries who have left us examples of this instruction were probably here following a model which may well go back to the period of the New Testament.[2]

It is in this context of the preaching of baptism that one must situate the doctrinal controversies which arose. This is the context which they presuppose and to which they belong. The dominating figure in the West in this emergence of baptismal doctrine, as in so many other areas, was St. Augustine. The controversies that marked his life, especially those with the Donatists and the Pelagians, forced him to think deeply on sacramental questions and especially on baptism. The doctrine of baptism in the Western Church is mainly a systematization of this teaching of St. Augustine.

[1]For the doctrine and theology of baptism, see: B. Neunheuser, *Baptism and Confirmation* (London: Burns & Oates, 1964, trans. from German); B. Leeming, *Principles of Sacramental Theology* (London: Longmans, Green, 1956); P. Pourrat, *Theology of the Sacraments* (London & St. Louis: Herder, 1930, trans. from French); L. Brockett, *The Theology of Baptism* (Cork: Mercier, 1971).

[2]See E. Yarnold, *op. cit.*

The first baptismal controversy was a very basic one. It arose because heretical sects, cut off from the Church, continued to administer baptism as their own initiation rite. This posed the question for the Church of the status of this rite. Was this a true baptism or merely its outward semblance, a mere imitation? Could there be true baptism outside the Church or was baptism confined within the Church, to the Church's own practice? This question arose as early as the second century. From the beginning the Church had no doubt that baptism was the rite of entry into its own ranks and therefore did not belong to any other group. Baptism was a rite of the Church and belonged to the Church. This insistence led logically enough to the position adopted by St. Cyprian in North Africa in the middle of the third century when this question became a public issue practically involving the whole Church. St. Cyprian found himself faced with the question concerning those baptized in heresy who now wished to become members of the Church. Should such converts be baptized again or not? Cyprian's position on this issue was quite clear: baptism conferred outside the Church has no value whatever and such converts must now be properly baptized in the Church. This North African position found strong support from the East. But Rome adopted a more subtle position. It maintained that its own practice was that, if the baptism had been duly performed, that is, in accordance with the Church's prescriptions and practice, then it should not be repeated. Such converts should be received into the Church by a special penitential ceremony for the reception and reconciliation of heretics. Though in this dispute, known as the Rebaptism Controversy, the theological arguments seemed to be on Cyprian's side, it was the Roman position which eventually came to be accepted throughout the Church. A satisfactory theoretical solution, however, had to await the intervention of St. Augustine at the beginning of the fifth century.

THE INFLUENCE OF ST. AUGUSTINE

Though this precise issue was no longer a live one in Augustine's time, it arose under another form. The strong Donatist sect in North Africa maintained that only a holy or worthy minister could truly celebrate the sacraments and since it regarded all the ministers of the Catholic Church as sinners, it consequently rejected the Church's baptism as valueless. Augustine was quick to see that a very basic issue was in question here. The Donatist position made the very existence and reality of a sacrament depend upon the interior, subjective disposition of the celebrating minister. But since this disposition was in itself ultimately unknowable, except to God alone, no one could ever be sure whether what purported to be a sacrament was such or not. Augustine saw very clearly that what was at stake here was the objective existence and reality of the Church's sacraments.

Augustine countered the Donatist position by maintaining that the true minister of baptism was not the human minister but the living Christ acting through the human minister. Where the rite of baptism was properly performed in accordance with the Church's practice and intention, there Christ himself was acting and the sacrament of baptism existed, irrespective of the personal merits or demerits of the human minister. Baptism could, therefore, truly exist and be received outside the Catholic Church in the heretical sects. If those so baptized later wished to be received into the Catholic Church, they should be received, not by being baptized again, but by the rite for the reconciliation of heretics. But while recognising that baptism could exist in heresy outside the Church, Augustine denied that such a baptism could have any spiritual effect or fruit. Sins were not here forgiven nor any grace conferred. This was an implication of the accepted view of the time that profession of heresy was formally wilful and sinful. The sin of heresy, therefore, acted as a barrier against the heretical baptism bearing any spiritual fruit. The spiritual and sanctifying effects proper to baptism could only be realized when the sin of heresy was acknowledged and truly repented of in the reception of the person into the Catholic Church.

This position of Augustine on the question of baptism outside the Church rests on two basic points. The first is that the real minister of baptism is Christ himself and that he can act through human instruments even outside the visible Church. The second is that a distinction must be made between the existence of baptism as such and its spiritual effect or fruit: the former can exist without the latter.

Augustine argued his case with clarity and force and this theological defence of the Church's practice eventually became standard doctrine. The distinction between the mere existence of baptism and its spiritual effect or fruit became the distinction between the validity and efficacy of the sacrament. This distinction forced Augustine to consider the circumstances where the distinction was verified, that is, the minimum conditions which had to be met for the sacrament of baptism merely to exist. His reply was that baptism truly existed where its *sacramentum* or outward sign, that is, the essential rite, had been properly performed. This essential rite he described as consisting of two elements, the washing with water and the accompanying word, that is, the credal confession of faith which accompanied the immersion, though he may have had a wider context in mind here in this concept of *verbum*. In other words, where the essential elements of the Church's practice were followed and performed, the baptism was valid, it truly existed and could not be repeated, whether or not the sacrament also had its intended spiritual effect. This spiritual effect of the sacrament Augustine defined, in line with tradition, in both negative and positive terms. Negatively, baptism effected the forgiveness of sins, both original sin and all actual personal sins, and, positively, it conferred the grace of union with Christ and participation in his relationship with the Father in the Spirit. This membership and discipleship of Christ also meant membership of the Church, the body of Christ. In the light of all these considerations, Augustine was able to clarify the question of the minister of baptism, vindicating the traditional position of the Church which was, in effect, that while the bishop and his delegated

ministers were the proper and normal ministers of the sacrament, anyone, or at least any Christian, who performed the
ceremony properly baptized validly.

The basic distinctions which Augustine made between the
outward sign, the grace and the minister of baptism enabled
him also to throw light on other doctrinal aspects and
implications of the sacrament. It had always been the
unquestioned tradition of the Church that a real or valid
baptism could not be repeated, it could be conferred and
received only once. Once Augustine had made his distinction between the mere existence of the sacrament and its
spiritual effect of grace, and had shown that the former
could exist without the latter, he found himself forced to
recognise another effect of the sacrament distinct from
grace, an effect that was automatic once the sacrament
existed. If baptism could be received only once and yet not
be accompanied by its appropriate spiritual effect, then
obviously it had some automatic, permanent effect distinct
from grace which explained its unrepeatability. Augustine
identified this effect as a marking of the recipient, a character as he termed it, which proclaimed him a member, even if
a defective one, of Christ and of the body of Christ, the
Church. We have here the origin of the doctrine of the
sacramental character which later will also be extended to
confirmation and holy orders. What Augustine had in mind
can most easily be described as the conferring of a *status*, the
status of being a Christian, of belonging to Christ and
membership of the Church. Though such status should
involve grace and the christian virtues, the fruits of discipleship, it can anomalously exist without them. The sinner
does not cease to be a Christian simply because he is a
sinner. This defective condition can be remedied only when
the sin which is obstructing the grace of the sacrament has
been repented of and removed. Only then does the anomaly
cease and the sacrament and its spiritual effect co-exist.

The question of the necessity of baptism for salvation was
another important issue where Augustine's influence was to
be significant, if not altogether happy. Here again he inherited a traditional position on the part of the Church which,

on the basis of texts such as Mark 16:16, saw the reception of baptism, that is, of being formally a Christian, as a necessary condition for salvation, though it also recognised that baptism of blood, the martyr's death, or baptism of desire could substitute here for the actual sacrament. Augustine fully endorsed this understanding but his treatment of the question was further determined by his sombre concept of original sin. Because of original sin mankind as such was a *massa damnata*, a condemned mass. Salvation was possible only as the pure gift and grace of God. God offered this grace to man in Christ but it requires of man that he establish saving union with Christ through faith. Baptism is where this union with Christ is established. Baptism is therefore necessary for salvation, though Augustine also recognises the surrogates of baptism of blood and of desire.

This teaching of Augustine on original sin and his situating the question of the necessity of baptism for salvation in this context, led him to stress the importance of infant baptism in a way the Church had never previously done, as he himself was a living witness, since he was not baptized until he was thirty-three. Infants, being children of Adam, were infected with original sin and belonged to the *massa damnata*. Because of this, if they died before receiving baptism, they died at enmity with God and were damned, though Augustine granted, generously enough, that their punishment would only involve the lightest of pain. The practical consequence of this analysis was obvious: infants should be baptized as soon as possible after birth. The strong emphasis on the early baptism of infants, which developed in subsequent centuries, had its origin in this Augustinian doctrinal synthesis.

Another aspect of infant baptism also bothered the great African bishop and led him to make another lasting contribution to the Church's doctrinal understanding of the sacrament. Baptism accomplished the convert's saving union with Christ through faith and it constituted his formal profession of faith in Christ. Baptism was the sacrament of faith. An infant, however, was incapable of such a profession of faith. How, then, could an infant receive the sacrament of baptism? In addressing himself to this question Augustine was not concerned with the practice of infant baptism as such. This was already established, a long-standing tradition in the Church. Augustine was concerned with the theoretical problem which the practice involved, the problem how a subject incapable of a personal act of faith could be a proper subject for the sacrament of faith. His solution to this question was that here the Church itself, especially through the parents and sponsors, acted as proxy for the infant, professing faith in its name and thereby going guarantor to nurture this child in the faith of the community until it was able to make its own the faith professed in its name at baptism. This position became and has remained the traditional answer of the Church to this question.

THE MEDIEVAL SYNTHESIS:
ST. THOMAS AQUINAS

The theological issues concerning baptism which Augustine addressed and his solutions to these questions became in the centuries after him the basis of the Church's teaching on the sacrament and of its presentation in systematic theology. Systematic treatment requires that the component elements of a subject be distinguished and separately considered. Only then can the unity of the whole be understood. Augustine's discussion of baptismal questions laid the foundation for such an approach to the theology of baptism. He distinguished such different elements as the outward sign, the effects, the minister, the recipient of the sacrament and in one way or another discussed the issues which arose with regard to each of these. It only required these distinct discussions to be linked together for a systematic theological treatise of baptism to emerge. This was the special achievement of the medieval scholastics. Sacramental theology was a prominent topic in medieval theology, and especially in the Paris schools of the twelfth and thirteenth centuries. General sacramental principles were worked out and this further helped the development of a systematic treatment of individual sacraments. Augustine's teaching on baptism and the implications of that teaching were here elaborated into a considerable body of baptismal theology.

The fruit of this labour can be best seen in St. Thomas Aquinas' treatment of baptism in Part Three of his great work, *Summa Theologiae.* Aquinas devotes six Questions, Questions 66-71, to the sacrament. The separate topics discussed in these Questions quickly reveal the stamp of Augustine and his influence on western sacramental theology. They are, in order: the external sign, the minister, the recipient, the effects, the rites, and, finally, catechism and exorcism. The last two topics, namely, the rites, catechism and exorcism, show that a consciousness of the old solemn process of christian initiation had not totally disappeared by the thirteenth century. But Aquinas' basic discussion of the theological issues of baptism is contained in the first four topics. Here he follows the standard line of medieval theology, which is thoroughly Augustinian, but with some further precisions.

The medieval theology of baptism began with the question of the outward form of the sacrament, Augustine's *sacramentum* or visible sign. By the thirteenth century medieval theology was discussing this question in terms of the Aristotelian concepts of matter and form, where "matter" referred to the essential action to be performed and "form" to the essential accompanying words. These words determined the meaning of the action and gave it its sacramental significance. It was easy to put this construction on Augustine's description of the outward form of baptism: the "matter" here was the cleansing with water, the "form" the words said by the minister while pouring the water. For some centuries now these words were not the credal questions and responses of the ancient rite but the indicative statement: "I baptise N. in the name of the Father and of the Son and of the Holy Spirit". The medievals were thinking here of the minimum action and words required for the existence of the sacrament and of the form of the sacrament as it existed in their own time. They had little realization of the solemn ceremony of christian initiation in the ancient church and little knowledge of the historical developments which had occurred in the liturgy of baptism. They consequently think of the celebration of the sacrament of baptism in terms much narrower than Augustine and their use of the concepts of matter and form only emphasises this difference between the ancient church and the medieval.[3]

Medieval theology paid close attention to Augustine's teaching on the effects of baptism, and especially to his distinction between the grace effect of the sacrament and the sacramental character. Aquinas was able to use the fruits of this theology in his discussion of the effects of baptism, and especially on the sacramental character he made a signifcant contribution.

The grace which baptism confers is the grace of redemption, of sharing in the redemption which Christ has accomplished. In speaking of this redemption, the biblical and patristic writers had presented it in personal terms, in terms of reconciliation and union with God through Christ in the Spirit. This personal and trinitarian approach suited the salvation history perspective of the Bible and the liturgy. But the beginning of a more ontological understanding can be discerned both in the, mainly Greek, concept of redemption as divinization and in Augustine's use of the concept of nature in his discussion of grace. The medievals developed this ontological approach and, applying Aristotelian concepts, presented grace as a new quality of the soul which elevated it to a supernatural level, a state of union with God as he is in himself, a creatural participation in the divine nature. This is the understanding of grace which Aquinas presents and this is how he sees the grace which baptism confers. The grace of baptism, its sanctifying, spiritual fruit, is the grace of redemption in Christ. It involves the forgiveness of sins, original and actual, and reconciliation and union with God through the infusion of this new quality which elevates the soul to union with God and participation

---

[3]On the difference between the patristic and medieval understanding of sacrament, see T. Marsh, "The History of the Sacramental Concept," *Milltown Studies* 3(1979), 21-55.

in his life or being. This also involves for the soul the giving or infusion of the theological virtues of faith, hope, and charity and the indwelling of the Holy Spirit with his gifts and fruits. This grace, Aquinas insists, is a participation in the grace with which the humanity of Christ was itself endowed in the Incarnation. It is the grace of union with Christ as Head of his Body, the redeemed humanity which is his Church. With this emphasis Aquinas maintains the personal and communal dimensions of grace which this ontological approach might otherwise lack.

The question of the sacramental character was a much discussed topic in medieval sacramental theology. Aquinas presents his mature views on this question in the *Summa*, though he discusses the matter most fully in his tract on the sacraments in general rather than when discussing the individual sacraments concerned (*S. Th.* III, q. 73). Augustine when treating of the character which baptism conferred had stressed the baptized's status as a Christian, a member of Christ. The baptized were marked with the sign of Christ and so belonged to him. In line with the medieval tradition Aquinas also sees the character as an indelible spiritual mark on the soul which establishes and proclaims membership of Christ, the status of being a Christian. But he also realizes that membership of Christ is realized and expressed through membership of the christian community. The character which baptism confers refers, therefore, also to membership of the Church and participation in its life. From his study of the Epistle to the Hebrews Aquinas found a way in the context of the sacramental character to integrate these two notions of membership of Christ and membership of the Church. The main topic of Hebrews is the priesthood of Christ as exercised in his once-for-all sacrifice on the cross. To be a member of Christ means to share in this priesthood, to be united with him in his dedicatory relationship to his Father, in his giving to and receiving from the Father. It is this relationship of Son to Father which constitutes and is celebrated in the Church's liturgical worship, especially the sacramental liturgy. The sacramental character of baptism in making one a member of Christ, a Christian, gives participation in this priesthood of Christ and thereby enables and deputes one to participate in this worship of the Church. For Aquinas the baptismal character confers the status of membership of Christ and of the Church and is the source of the common priesthood of the faithful which is a participation in the priesthood of Christ.

By the time of Aquinas the question of the minister of baptism was no longer a point of contention. Augustine's position that personal worthiness, though desirable, was not a requisite in the minister and that the minister was simply an instrument of Christ and the Church had by now become established doctrine. Aquinas simply represents his time in asserting that anyone, a lay-person or even a non-Christian, could be a minister of baptism provided they perform properly the matter and form and do so with a "right intention". This intention is described as the intention "to do what the Church does", that is, to act, explicitly or implicitly, as a minister of the Church in this action.

Concerning the recipient of the sacrament Aquinas' position is again the traditional one. Baptism is necessary for salvation but baptism of desire or of blood will also suffice. When the candidate is an adult, faith and an intention to receive the sacrament are required for the sacrament to be valid. On the question of infant baptism Aquinas insists infants should be baptized and then considers the question of faith in this case. The medievals spoke of the infusion of the virtue of faith as an effect of the sacrament, even in the unconscious infant, and many saw in this the faith required for the sacrament in the case of infants. Aquinas, however, is conscious that a more existential basis is required and he supports Augustine's view that here the Church itself supplies for the faith of the infant by professing its own faith in its name. Realistically, Aquinas sees the parents as the particular representatives of the Church here and attributes a primary role to their faith. Having given the infant existence, so now they also commit themselves to giving it their faith which is the faith of the Church.

LIMITATIONS AND RENEWAL

Medieval sacramental theology found its most impressive statement in Aquinas' presentation. It is not surprising, therefore, that in subsequent centuries when the Church needed a doctrinal statement on sacraments it had recourse to this thomistic synthesis. This was the case with the Decree for the Armenians issued by the Council of Florence in 1439, which included an important section on the sacraments based on the theology of St. Thomas. The same was again true at the Council of Trent in the sixteenth century. Trent's sacramental doctrine is thoroughly thomistic. Baptism, however, was not a major concern at Trent and the sacrament does not figure prominently in the Council's statements. It simply issued some Canons on the sacrament which were directed against certain statements of Luther which seemed to deny the sacramental status of baptism and to present it rather as a mere symbol and confirmation of faith. But Trent's great reliance on Aquinas' sacramental teaching further enhanced the prestige of this theology and ensured its prominent and indeed dominant position in catholic theology. As a result, the treatment of baptism in modern theological textboks has been very largely a representation of Aquinas. One finds in these works not only the same content but also the same form of presentation as that of the Summa. Baptism is usually discussed under the headings: Outward Sign, Effects, Minister, Recipient. This is the medieval format of the theology of baptism but behind it can be easily detected the influence of St. Augustine and the baptismal issues with which he was concerned.

In assessing the adequacy of this theology, it is necessary to bear in mind that not everything which theology has to say about baptism is included in the formal treatise devoted to the sacrament. While what theology studies is one organic whole, it has to perform its task in a piecemeal fashion, isolating certain aspects from the whole and discussing these separately. Topics such as christology, redemption, ecclesiology, sacraments thus form distinct studies. A disadvantage of this practically necessary approach is that the connection between these topics and their relation to the whole may often remain obscure. The theology of baptism has not escaped this fate. The questions this theology came to discuss were determined by the disputes which arose concerning the sacrament. These disputes certainly raised issues which any theology of baptism would have to face and consider. But these questions do not constitute a full theology of baptism. Many aspects of the sacrament did not figure in these controversies and are therefore not represented in the theology constructed from them. Other questions relevant to baptism were discussed in the other areas of theology. Such questions as union with Christ in the paschal mystery of his death and resurrection, the redemptive significance of this union, membership of the Church, the life of discipleship, such questions would be treated in the treatises on redemption, grace, the Church, and in moral theology. Moreover, it has to be remembered that the disputed questions which gave rise to the baptism tract presupposed the preaching of baptism in the Church and the broad presentation of the sacrament which this involved.

Nevertheless, the fact remains that this theology is more one of Special Questions than a comprehensive treatment of baptism. This became more and more true with the passing of time according as the old context of christian initiation with the instruction on baptism which went with it faded into the remote past. With this development these questions lost the rich context of which they were a part, the Church's understanding of baptism as celebrated in its solemn liturgy of initiation and constantly presented in its catechumenal and mystagogical catechesis. Eventually, these questions came to constitute *the* theology of baptism. Torn from their old context, they came to form a narrow, abstract study dealing with questions which seldom touched real life or had practical application. We have seen how the solemn celebration of baptism had become reduced by the Middle Ages to a very private, individualist inexpressive ceremony which scarcely touched the life of the christian community. This narrow experience of the rite and event of baptism also affected theological thought. The questions discussed were now seen in this context and thereby became themselves narrowed in outlook. This is particularly obvious in the discussion on the outward sign of the sacrament. If this question is seen in the context of the solemn celebration of baptism at the Easter Vigil, then the whole ritual has to enter the perspective of the question, even if the issue of the minimum essential rite has also to be considered. Justice is certainly not done to the rite if it is considered simply in terms of matter and form as the medievals and their modern representatives presented it. But these concepts fitted the contemporary experience of the sacrament and so passed unquestioned. A similar criticism can be levelled at the other sections of the tract. Questions concerning the effects, the minister and the recipient of the sacrament were discussed almost exclusively in terms of fringe cases concerning minimum requirements and efficacy. This rendered the study abstract and remote from the ordinary life and experience of the Church. The absence from the discussion of biblical and liturgical perspectives only emphasised still further this abstract character. The whole study gave the impression of a canonical rather than a theological tract.

It has only been in this century that a realization of these inadequacies in the traditional theology of baptism has developed. New studies, especially in the areas of the history of religion, the New Testament, liturgy and ritual, brought an awareness of many basic dimensions of the sacrament which had no place in the older presentation. These new perspectives have led to a new and more comprehensive appreciation of baptism which has not remained purely academic but which has sought practical and pastoral application. The liturgical and theological renewal initiated by Vatican II has sanctioned and given direction to this effort to implement this new understanding. In the next chapter we will look at the form and implications of this renewal which is now under way in the Church.

The Question of Confirmation

The official doctrine of the Church on the sacrament of confirmation can be briefly stated. The Council of Trent declared it "a true and proper sacrament", one of the seven sacraments of the New Law. Over a century earlier a fuller statement had been issued by the Council of Florence in its Decree for the Armenians in 1439.[4] The teaching of this statement may be summarised as follows:

in confirmation there is a giving of the Spirit;

this gift represents the perpetuation of Pentecost in the Church;

it is directed towards the public profession and witness of the faith;

it involves a strengthening of the Christian for this mission.

This statement is based on St. Thomas Aquinas' theology of confirmation and represents a summary of it. His discussion of confirmation was the fullest and clearest which the Middle Ages produced. It constitutes a brilliant and penetrating analysis of the theological tradition on this sacrament as this was known to him in the thirteenth century. In basing its statement on Aquinas the Council of Florence acknowledges the merit of this theology and gives it official status. Since then, this statement has come to represent the Church's official understanding of confirmation and is the position represented in theological and religious instruction works down to our own time. It can be recognised again in Vatican II in the comment on confirmation in *Lumen Gentium* II.

> Reborn as sons of God, they (the faithful) must confess before men the faith which they have received from God through the Church. Bound more intimately to the Church by the sacrament of confirmation, they are endowed by the Holy Spirit with special strength. Hence they are more strictly obliged to spread and defend the

[4]See J. Neuner & J. Dupuis, eds., *The Christian Faith in the Doctrinal Documents of the Catholic Church* (Dublin & Cork, Mercier, 1973) 370-372.

faith both by word and by deed as true witnesses of Christ.

The adequacy of this understanding of confirmation, however, has remained a question. The meaning of the sacrament has been the subject of much discussion particularly in this century. To assess its theological adequacy, it is necessary to see this understanding in the context of the theological tradition from which it derives and of which it is a summary. This means going behind the statement to the theology of Aquinas which is its basis and to the sources and tradition which he sought to penetrate and formulate. The theology of Aquinas and the statement of the Council of Florence are a product of the history of the theology of confirmation in the West. Only this history can enable us to understand this theology and statement and assess their adequacy. But before engaging on this task, it may be helpful if we attempt first to state what precisely the question of confirmation is.

THE QUESTION

The statement that one most frequently hears about confirmation today is that it is a problem, a question. Upon further analysis, the problem proves to be manifold and complex. The basic question certainly is the meaning and significance of this sacrament. This is especially the question of its distinction from and relation to baptism. If baptism has the rich significance which the teaching and practice of the Church ascribes to it, what further contribution can confirmation make to the life and status of the Christian? One of the more recent official statements on the meaning of baptism occurs in *Christian Initiation: General Introduction* issued with the Rite of Baptism of Children in 1969. In that document we read:

> Through baptism men and women are incorporated into Christ. They are formed into God's people, and they obtain forgiveness of all their sins ----- They become a

> new creation through water and the Holy Spirit. Hence
> they are called, and are indeed, the children of God.
> -----baptism is the sacrament by which men and women
> are incorporated into the Church, built into a house
> where God lives, in the Spirit, into a holy nation and a
> royal priesthood.

In effect, full participation in the life of the Church is
available to one who is baptized but not confirmed. Such a
one, granted the other necessary conditions, can validly
marry or even be ordained a priest or bishop. What further
meaning, then, can reception of confirmation have? Has it
any meaning?

Uncertainty on this central issue inevitably involves
uncertainty also in other areas. It gives rise to questions
concerning the celebration of confirmation and the pastoral
context of this ministry. At what age and in what circumstances should confirmation be conferred? How should the
candidates be prepared and instructed? These important
and very practical questions have been much discussed in
recent decades but there has been little sign of any generally
acceptable answers emerging. It seems that clarification of
the central theological issue is first required before a coherent and appropriate pastoral practice can develop. The one
is dependent on and awaits the other.

If one consults the theological sciences hoping to obtain
light on these various issues, one simply runs into further
problems. The evidence of the New Testament concerning a
post-baptismal rite for the gift of the Spirit is much disputed. Even the existence of such a rite is questioned. The
later history of the post-baptismal rites is also difficult to
reconstruct fully and there are a number of areas here which
still remain obscure. In some parts of the Church for certain
periods either no post-baptismal rite apparently existed or
the existence of a specific rite of the Spirit is questionable.
Uncertainty in these areas makes a reconstruction of the
history of the theology of confirmation very difficult and it
is scarcely surprising, therefore, that this history is also a
disputed question. Theology is very dependent on these

sources of scriptural interpretation and history and where the evidence of these sources is itself disputed, as in the case of confirmation, a coherent theology is difficult to construct.

The question of confirmation is thus many-sided and complex and efforts to resolve it face many problems. Yet, the picture is far from totally black. Despite the uncertainties and obscurities, a sufficient body of evidence does exist to enable the task of reconstruction and interpretation to be undertaken with a reasonable hope that a coherent picture will emerge which will throw light on those issues which constitute the question of confirmation. In this hope we turn now to this task of reconstructing the history of the theological understanding of confirmation.

HISTORY OF THEOLOGY[5]

We have seen earlier in this study that christian initiation, in and from its very origin, has always incorporated two basic references, a christological reference and a pneumatological reference. Throughout all the many forms which initiation has taken in different times and places over the centuries, this has remained a constant. One may therefore well regard this double reference as defining christian initiation. Christian initiation means entering into union with Christ in the power of the Spirit.

The reason why this double reference came to exist and to be so basic is to be found in the concepts and themes of biblical salvation history. The promise made to Israel, constituting them the People of God, looked forward to a fulfilment to be inaugurated by the messianic bringer of salvation and involving as its crowning gift the eschatological gift of God's Spirit. The Christian Church was born from the faith that in the person and history of Jesus of Nazareth this fulfilment had occurred. The community of the disciples of Jesus, born of this faith, now existed as the possessor

[5]See T. Marsh, "A Study of Confirmation," *Irish Theological Quarterly* 39(1972), 149-163, 319-336; 40(1973), 125-147.

of the messianic blessings which the victory of Jesus had made available. To enter this community meant to share in its life as constituted by these blessings. It meant union with Christ and the gift of the Spirit. Entry into the community was accomplished through a ritual expression. A rite of water, baptism, expressed and realized the union with Christ which membership of the community involved; similarly, the rite of imposition of hands, after baptism, expressed and realized the giving of the Spirit. Christian initiation involved these two rites because the two themes of Messiah and the gift of Spirit were essentially distinct and separate in the thought of Judaism. In terms of sequence of events, one was seen as following the other; the general gift of the Spirit followed as a result of the work of the Messiah. To the minds of the first Christians, this projected pattern matched their actual experience. As historical events their experience of the outpouring of the Spirit followed their experience of Jesus of Nazareth. The shape of christian initiation in its original form was determined by this mental outlook and historical experience. Thus placed in its historical context, this ritual was totally logical.

Problems, however, soon emerged with this form of christian initiation. The rite of cleansing with water aptly expressed the washing away of sins, which was a central aspect of the messianic blessings strongly emphasized in the imagery of the prophets. Imposition of hands was an established Jewish rite expressing participation in the spirit of the community, in this case the presence of the Spirit of God. But forgiveness of sins was a negative concept understood in Judaism as a cancelling of debts. It did not adequately express the positive aspects of the messianic redemption, the renewal of heart of which Ezechiel had spoken. On the other hand, the concept of the Spirit in early Christianity was, inevitably, that of contemporary Judaism. But this was the concept of the prophetic Spirit, the Spirit as source of revelation, of forceful preaching, confirming signs and charismatic action. In itself, this concept was distinct from forgiveness of sins and the positive element of renewal of heart. It presupposed these and followed them as a crowning, sealing gift. The original form of christian initiation, with the two rites expressing the two basic references, revealed a lacuna here in christian thought which would have to be filled. Moreover, while the two rites were certainly meant to relate the two references and not to separate them, the distinction inevitably raised the question of such a separation. This created the anomalous situation where union with Christ (baptism) was conceivable without a sharing in the Spirit of Christ (imposition of hands), a situation verified in the Samaria episode before the arrival of the Apostles. Christian reflection would also have to deal with this anomaly.

What we find emerging in these problems is the limitations of the salvation history model for religious understanding. This model, since it thinks in terms of discrete time and events in time, is not able to do justice to the transcendent unity which comes to historical expression in these events. This unity is what theological thought seeks. Almost from the beginning, therefore, there was a tension between this theological effort of the christian mind and the pattern of christian initiation determined by the salvation history model and experience, the former striving to impose a coherent unity on the discrete references of the latter.

The most notable effort in early Christianity to resolve this tension, in the area of christian initiation, was that of St. Paul. We have already discussed his achievement here and how he came to it. The basic original insight which led him to his synthesis was his retrieval of the concept of the Spirit as *life-giving*. This enabled him to integrate the themes of Christ and Spirit, to see Christ as Lord in terms of the life-giving Spirit and union with Christ as sharing in his Spirit. In this way he forges a unity between the two references and rites of christian initiation and can now present this complex process as a unity. Further, this enables him to fill the lacuna in christian initiation due to the absence of reference to the positive aspects of union with Christ. This can now be expressed in terms of the life-giving Spirit accomplishing this union with Christ, giving participation in his life and directing the living out of this life in discipleship. The Spirit giving life in Christ is thus the power operating in baptism and accomplishing its effects. The different elements of christian initiation here attain an integration and coherent unity.

The history of early christian literature, at least until Irenaeus of Lyons (d.c. 200), reveals that Paul's advanced theological thought made little impact on the general christian understanding. St. Luke is an outstanding early example of this, but even in the writings of the second century, until Irenaeus, the influence of Paul is conspicuous by its absence. One particular factor militating against the Pauline theology was precisely its high pneumatology. In early Christianity the theme of the Spirit was associated especially with the charismatic elements and experiences which constituted so notable a feature of the early Church. With the passage of time this feature regressed, while, correspondingly, institutional elements developed to direct and structure the life of the Church in a way inimical to the charismatic. With the fading of charismatic elements, consciousness of the Spirit, associated with this experience, faded also. The later documents of the New Testament already illustrate this. In many of these there is scarcely a significant reference to the Spirit. Further, conservative Jewish-Christian groups, still an influential body in the Church, reacted negatively to Paul's whole theological position and his free overtures to Gentiles which went with it. Since Paul in this outlook had opposed the Spirit to the Law, this reaction took the form of largely ignoring the theme of the Spirit which Paul had developed so dangerously. The Church's sharp reaction to Montanism, a Spirit-movement of the mid second century, may be said to mark the nadir of the theology of the Spirit in early Christianity.

It was at this period that the Gnostic movement began to pose its threat to the Church and it profited from the neglect of the Spirit which had now come to characterise much of christian life and thought. Christian Gnosticism, or at least significant branches of it, claimed to be the Church of the Spirit and sought to win adherents from the Great Church on this ground. The low pneumatology which now generally prevailed left the Church especially vulnerable to this attack. It was now that Irenaeus, seeking to defend the Church from the Gnostic threat, saw the point and value of Paul's theology of the Spirit. The Spirit of God possessed the Church and was the source of its whole life: "Where the Church is, there is the Spirit of God, and where the Spirit of God is, there is the Church and every kind of grace". (*Adversus Haereses* 4,33,9). Irenaeus here initiates the revival of Pauline thought which will come to fruition in the great writers of the fourth century.[6]

This weakening of a consciousness of the Spirit, the threat felt even by appeal to this concept, and then the Gnostic challenge precisely on this ground, all these factors came together around the middle of the second century. It is quite likely, I think, that the later Syrian initiation liturgy, which we briefly discussed earlier, had its origin from this complex situation. There the post-baptismal rite of the Spirit disappeared and the pneumatological reference to initiation came to be associated particularly with the pre-baptismal anointing. But apart from this development, neither the Pauline theology itself, on the one hand, nor the low pneumatology which developed in the Church, on the other, affected the existence and continuance of the original pattern of christian initiation. This is certainly true of the West where Tertullian in North Africa and Hippolytus at Rome are clear witnesses of a form of initiation substantially the same as that found in the Acts of the Apostles. But now an important new feature begins to emerge.

According as, following the lead of Irenaeus, the Pauline theology of the Spirit, as animating the life of the Church and the Christian, develops, the Spirit comes to be seen as the source of the sanctifying power of the sacraments. The epiclesis of the Spirit in baptism, at the blessing of the water, and in the eucharist now begin to appear. We now find the

---

[6]On the understanding of the Spirit in early Christianity, see my article "The Holy Spirit in Early Christian Teaching," *Irish Theological Quarterly*, 45(1978), 101-116.

sanctifying effects of baptism presented as the work of the life-giving Spirit operating in this sacrament, a sure sign we are again in the Pauline perspective. A pneumatological reference is thus here inserted into baptism itself. This, however, did not affect the continuance of the post-baptismal rite with its formal assertion of the gift of the Spirit. There has now developed, therefore, an understanding which sees a double pneumatological reference in christian initiation, one in baptism, associated with the sanctifying operation of the Spirit, filling that lacuna mentioned earlier, and another in the traditional context of the post-baptismal rite.

Two observations on this development are relevant here. Reference to the role of the Spirit in baptism occurs in comment on the rite; it is not inserted into the rite itself, apart from the epiclesis over the water. Thus, for example, the classical Roman rite of baptism, apart from the water blessing, contains no significant reference to the Spirit. The rite itself retains its primitive interpretation and remains unaffected by the theological development. Further, the special terminology associated with the gift of the Spirit, for example, "being filled with" the Spirit, is almost always, in the West, reserved to the context of the post-baptismal rite.

Tertullian, in his work *On Baptism*, provides an interesting and early illustration of this awkward co-existence of the two pneumatological references in christian initiation. In that work we find the following statements concerning baptism.

> The guilt being removed, of course the penalty is removed too. Thus, man will be restored for God to his 'likeness' ---- for he receives again that Spirit of God which he had then first received from his afflatus (in-breathing) but had afterwards lost through sin ---- Not that in the waters we obtain the Holy Spirit; but in the water under (the influence of) the angel, we are cleansed, and (thus) prepared for the Holy Spirit. ---- In the next place the hand is laid on us, invoking and inviting the Holy Spirit through (the words of) benediction. ---- Then, on our cleansed and

blessed bodies willingly descends from the Father that Holiest Spirit.[7]

Tertullian is here on the point of asserting a gift of the Spirit both in baptism and in the imposition of hand. The concept of the Spirit he wishes to see in baptism is the life-giving Spirit referred to in Genesis 2:7, the source of the new life in Christ given in baptism. At the same time he realizes that he cannot abandon the explicit assertion of the gift of the Spirit in the post-baptismal rite. He is forced into an incoherent position, but the incoherence is understandable in the light of the groping theological effort which is now under way and which he here illustrates.

This attribution of the sanctifying effects of baptism to the Spirit becomes a major theme in the baptismal theology of the christian writers of the fourth century. The text of John 3:5, on the necessity of being born "of water and of the Spirit", here becomes an important and much referred to text. A number of writers now begin to point out that Christ twice gave the Spirit, adding together the accounts of the event in John 20:22-23 and Acts 2, the Johannine and Lucan Pentecosts.[8] St. Augustine noted the relevance of this assertion to christian initiation and he explicitly asserts *two* gifts of the Spirit in initiation, corresponding to the two Gospel accounts, one in baptism and the other through the imposition of hand.[9] This assertion of two gifts of the Spirit, which is going to be very influential later in the West, has to be situated and seen in the context of the patristic catechesis and commentary on christian initiation. This followed the lines of the salvation history perspective of the biblical presentation. In particular, it saw and used the baptism of Jesus as a paradigm of christian initiation. Here there was

[7]*On Baptism*, 5:7; 6:1; 8:1. Translation from *Ante-Nicene Christian Library* (Edinburgh, T. & T. Clark, 1892), eds. A. Roberts and J. Donaldson, Vol. 11: The Writings of Tertullian, Vol. 1.

[8]See Eusebius, *On Ecclesiastical Theology*, 3:5; Gregory of Nazianzus, *On Pentecost*, 9:11; Cyril of Jerusalem, *Catecheses* 17:12.

[9]Augustine, *On The Trinity*, 15:46; *Sermon*, 71:19; *Sermon* 265:7.

the actual baptism with which could be associated the heavenly voice proclaiming Jesus' divine sonship. This provided an appropriate basis for developing the christological reference and implications of baptism. The coming of the Spirit upon Jesus after his baptism then provided a context from which to explain the post-baptismal pneumatological reference of initiation. The structure of this whole context paralleled that of the full initiation rite and provided an excellent basis for relating the themes of initiation with the life of Christ and the role of the Spirit in that life and in the life of the Church.

The theology which came to associate the Spirit with baptism as agent of its effects saw the Spirit active here in his life-giving aspect. The concept of the life-giving Spirit thus now comes to be attached to baptism. The christological reference of baptism is here again integrated, as in Paul, with this concept of the Spirit. But now the post-baptismal gift of the Spirit has to be distinguished from this baptismal role. The distinction is ready to hand in the concept of the prophetic Spirit. This is the concept which characterises especially the presentation of the Spirit in Luke, in both the Gospel and Acts. Especially, it is the concept presented in those passages which describe or make reference to the gift of the Spirit after baptism. The Spirit which comes on Jesus at the Jordan is the sustaining source of his ministry of preaching and miracles. This is the Spirit which Christ promises to his followers (Luke 12:11-12; 21:12-17; Acts 1:8; cf. Matt. 10:17-21; 24:9,13; Mark 13:9-11). This promise is fulfilled for the Church at Pentecost and then extended to new members in the post-baptismal rite of christian initiation. The marks of forceful preaching and confirming signs which characterised this role of the Spirit in the ministry of Jesus are here extended to the Church and consistently accompany the gift of the Spirit in Luke's presentation.

There was here a rich field of New Testament, and especially Lucan, material which could be appealed to as a basis for presenting the post-baptismal gift of the Spirit as the prophetic Spirit active in the Church. The salvation history approach of the Fathers in their preaching on christian initiation leads them to follow this rhythm of the scriptural passages which illustrate their theme. Seeing the life-giving Spirit at work in baptism, in the post-baptismal context they concentrate on the prophetic aspect of the Spirit and appeal to the biblical context of this concept. We see here how the gift of the Spirit is being divided between the two poles of christian initiation, baptism and the post-baptismal rite. Tertullian had already found his thought moving in this direction but was unable to develop it coherently. Later writers are able to overcome this problem through a clearer grasp of the distinction between the life-giving and prophetic roles of the Spirit as presented in the Bible, both the Old and the New Testament. This is the patristic tradition which St. Augustine inherits and which forms the background to his thought.

ST. AUGUSTINE

Augustine is the first to explicitly assert two gifts of the Spirit in christian initiation, in baptism and in the imposition of hand. He bases this assertion on the fact that Christ twice gave the Spirit, on Easter Sunday and again at Pentecost. On Easter Sunday the Spirit is given for the forgiveness of sins (John 20:22-23). This is a reference to baptism and the role of the Spirit here as agent of remission of sins and source of the regeneration spoken of in John 3:5. Augustine's understanding of the gift of the Spirit is determined above all by his favourite text, Romans 5:5: "God's love has been poured into our hearts through the Holy Spirit which has been given to us". The gift of the Spirit means God's love *in us*. This is the new life of baptism which transforms the old self and wipes out the sins of that past. But this love cannot remain isolated and imprisoned within the Christian. Of its essence love is outgoing. God's love in us is a missionary force which seeks to move out from us, to express itself, to permeate as an animating principle the whole christian body, the Body of Christ. Augustine traces the source of this missionary aspect of the gift of the Spirit to Pentecost and its sacramental continuation in the post-baptismal rite. This is his interpretation, in terms of his own personal theology, of the prophetic concept and role of the Spirit in the traditional catechesis. The charismatic elements so prominent in this salvation history approach are re-interpreted by him in terms of his master concept of charity and its source, the Holy Spirit. The gift which formerly manifested itself in signs such as the gift of tongues now expresses itself in the life of christian charity.

> Does it happen now with those on whom the hand is imposed for the reception of the Spirit that one expects them to speak in tongues? ----- If now the presence of the Spirit is not manifested by such miracles, how comes it, how does one know one has received the Spirit? Let him ask his own heart: if he loves the brother, the Spirit of God resides in him. Let him examine and prove himself in the sight of God, let him see if there is in him the love of peace and unity, the love of the Church spread throughout the whole world. (*In Epistolam Joannis*, 6,10).

Augustine asserts two gifts of the Spirit in christian initiation because, on the one hand, theological commentary on baptism has now given a central role to the Spirit in this sacrament, while, on the other, the traditional formal assertion of the gift of the Spirit in the post-baptismal rite still continues. In accordance with the general direction of patristic exegesis and commentary, Augustine also broadly distinguishes these two roles of the Spirit in terms of the life-giving and prophetic concepts of the Spirit. But he also attempts to discover an underlying unity here on the basis especially of Romans 5:5, with its reference to the Spirit given to us as the source of God's love in us and its dynamic force. With this concept of the Spirit as the principle of charity in the Church and its individual members, he attempts to bring together into one focus the two gifts which he asserts. Here again one notices the tension between the theological search for unity and the separate moments of the salvation history perspective. Sometimes Augustine's efforts are not convincing, as when he distinguishes the two gifts in terms of the double commandment of charity: the

Spirit given in baptism for the love of neighbour and after baptism for the love of God.[10] But this is not his central statement and his thought should not be judged on the basis of it. Overall, the thrust and enterprise of his thought is clear. He asserts two gifts of the Spirit in christian initiation and he seeks to give coherence to this assertion by discovering a unity and a distinction in the concept of the Spirit as the principle of charity.

Augustine's summing up and direction of the tradition he inherited on the role of the Spirit in initiation and his assertion of two gifts of the Spirit pass on to later generations as part of the great Augustinian legacy. This theology will later exercise a major influence in the West on the understanding of confirmation and its relation to baptism.

THE EARLY MIDDLE AGES[11]

As confirmation becomes separated from baptism in actual practice, the question of its meaning quickly becomes explicit and acute. While the old unified solemn ceremony of initiation prevailed, the question of the role of the Spirit in this process was not so explicit. Especially given the salvation history approach which the liturgy required, the Spirit could be viewed synthetically, as a coherent theme pervading the whole, rather than antithetically, in terms of stages contradistinguished from one another. But once confirmation has been separated from baptism by a significant interval of time, its independent existence calls for independent discussion and theology begins to ask what meaning attaches to this sacrament *over against* baptism.

The first to pose the question of confirmation in these terms was Faustus, bishop of Riez in Provence, sometime after the middle of the fifth century. It is clear from his statements that the separate administration of the sacraments had made the question topical. Faustus addressed

[10]*On the Trinity*, 15, 46; *Sermon*, 265:7.

[11]See J. D. C. Fisher, *Christian Initiation: Baptism in the Medieval West* (London: SPCK, 1965).

himself to the issue in a Pentecost sermon, taking as his text Acts 2:17 (= Joel 2:28), which in his text reads: "In those days, says the Lord, I will pour out my Spirit upon all flesh". He quickly comes to the point:[12]

> Because we say that the imposition of hand and confirmation has power to bestow something real upon him who has been born anew in Christ, possibly someone may think within himself: 'What good can it do me, after the sacrament of baptism, to have confirmation? So far as I can see, we have not obtained a fullness from the font, if after the font we still need the addition of something else.

In proceeding to answer his own question, Faustus distinguishes the two roles of the Spirit in christian initiation, at baptism and at confirmation.

> The Holy Spirit who came down upon the waters of baptism to bring salvation, bestows at the font all that is needed (*plenitudo*) for innocence; in confirmation he grants a development for progress (*augmentum*) in grace.

In seeing the Spirit active in both baptism and confirmation Faustus is but here repeating the by now established tradition. In baptism the Spirit is the author of the fullness of innocence which the sacrament confers, that is, forgiveness of sins and sanctification in Christ. But Faustus now proceeds to give an original and personal explanation of the role of the Spirit in confirmation. The Spirit is given again in this sacrament to develop and increase the grace given at baptism. This extra assistance is necessary because in living the christian life in the world the Christian has to face and overcome many difficulties and obstacles. The Spirit bestowed in confirmation provides this assistance. Thus Faustus can say, and indeed has to say, that for those who die immediately after baptism, confirmation is unnecessary.

---

[12]A critical edition of the text of this homily is provided by L. A. van Buchem, *L'Homelie Pseudo-Eusebienne de Pentecote* (Nijmegen, 1967). The translation given here is taken from B. Leeming, *op. cit.*, 624-5.

being now beyond the possibility of sinning, they are "confirmed by death". Only those who continue to live need this assistance. In Faustus' view confirmation is concerned with what later ages will call actual grace to avoid sin. This for him is the grace of confirmation, the purpose of this gift of the Spirit. This is a very moralistic view of the sacrament.

Faustus speaks of confirmation as a strengthening (*confirmatio, robur*) of the christian life given in baptism, a strengthening for the combat of life (*roboramur ad pugnam*). It is in this context that he introduces a military analogy to describe the relation between baptism and confirmation. Baptism is like the enrollment of the new recruit, confirmation represents the arming of the new soldier with his weapons. This is the source of that image of confirmation which speaks of it as making one "a soldier of Jesus Christ".

In the last chapter we saw how from the end of the fifth century through to the eighth the distinct episcopal rite of imposition of hand disappeared from the initiation liturgy over much of the West. Accordingly, such little reference as there is to confirmation in this period is found only in some Roman writers. But with the new dissemination of the Roman rite in the eighth century, a programme completed by the enterprise of Charlemagne and Alcuin, the abandoned rite is once again restored. With its reappearance in the liturgy, comment on the meaning of confirmation now begins again. The writers who now address the question pose it in much the same terms as Faustus. It is a question of the relation and the distinction between baptism and confirmation. The re-occurrence in this literature of Faustus' distinctive terminology of strengthening (*robur*) shows that his text has survived and exercises an influence. But what is significant is that his interpretation of this strengthening does not find favour. Those writers repeat Augustine's assertion of two gifts of the Spirit in christian initiation, in baptism and in confirmation. The Spirit is given in baptism as the source of regeneration, of new life in Christ — the Pauline concept of the life-giving Spirit again. The post-baptismal gift, on the other hand, is here interpreted in markedly and surprisingly explicit prophetic terms. Thus, Leidrad of Lyons, for example, at the end of the eighth century, commenting on the distinction between baptism and confirmation and the role of the Spirit in these sacraments, writes:

> in baptism the remission of sins is accomplished; in the imposition of hands gifts of charisms are conferred.[13]

But the most significant of the comments in this vein, and certainly the most explicit, is that of Alcuin himself. His statement is significant as a formulation of the issue at the time, as a source available to the later medieval period and as coming from one who, at the important school of Aachen, formed the minds of many of the influential ecclesiastics of the early ninth century. Alcuin would share the traditional view of the role of the Spirit in baptism. On the meaning of confirmation he writes, summarily, as follows:

> Last of all, through the imposition of hands by the chief priest (i.e., bishop) he receives the Spirit of sevenfold grace, so that he may be strengthened (*ut roboretur*) through the Holy Spirit to preach to others (*ad praedicandum aliis*), who was in baptism endowed by grace with eternal life.[14]

Baptism confers the grace of eternal life; in confirmation the Spirit is given for the preaching of the faith. With this succinct distinction Alcuin formulates with sharp insight the received tradition on the roles of the Spirit in christian initiation. Since it can be taken for granted that he would attribute, in accord with the established tradition, the effect of baptism to the Spirit, and since the reference to preaching cannot be a reference to any official or canonical mission, but rather to some special quality or power, it is clear that

---

[13] *Liber de Sacro Baptismo*, 7. I translate *dona virtutum* as "gifts of charisms."
[14] *Epistola* 134.

for him the Spirit operates in baptism as the source of the life it confers and in confirmation as a gift of prophetic force. This is a sharp formulation of the tradition which attributes a double role to the Spirit in the sacraments of initiation and distinguishes these roles in terms of the life-giving and prophetic concepts of the Spirit.

That this is a correct interpretation of Alcuin is placed beyond doubt by the comments some years later of one of his pupils, Rabanus Maurus. Rabanus explicitly asserts, in terms which show the influence of St. Augustine, two gifts of the Spirit in christian initiation. Though he discusses the first of these in the context of the baptismal anointing, this for him is a baptismal rite which theologically expresses the meaning of baptism. Theologically, therefore, there is question here of a baptismal gift of the Spirit. Then, in explaining the meaning of confirmation, Rabanus takes up again and expands the text of Alcuin.

> Finally, the Holy Spirit, the Comforter, is transmitted to him by the chief priest through the imposition of hand, that he may be strengthened (*ut roboretur*) through the Holy Spirit to preach to others the gift which he has himself gained in baptism, having been endowed through grace with eternal life. ----- The Holy Spirit now comes into the person, with this intent, that the seal of faith, which he has accepted on his brow, may make him replete with heavenly gifts (*donis coelestibus repletum*), and strengthened by his grace to bear the name of Christ fearlessly and boldly before kings and rulers of this world, and to preach it with a free voice.[15]

Rabanus simply reproduces here in expanded form the thought of his master. In doing so, however, he accurately sums up the long tradition, going back to the early Church itself, which understands the post-baptismal gift of the Spirit in prophetic terms, as ordained to forceful preaching

---

[15] *De Clericorum Institutione*, 1:30.

of the faith accompanied and confirmed by other signs of the Spirit's power (*donis coelestibus repletum*).

The commentary of the Carolingian writers on the meaning of confirmation thus adopts Faustus' terminology of strengthening, but they reject his moralistic understanding and explanation of this term. Rather, they use this term to express that prophetic quality which in the tradition characterises the gift of the Spirit in the post-baptismal rite of imposition of hand. They bring together in a coherent, succinct statement the strands of the tradition whose development we have been tracing and which seeks to understand and express the role of the Spirit in christian initiation. It was found necessary here to find a role for the Spirit in baptism, though the rite itself did not refer to this, apart from the epiclesis over the water which, as we have seen, was in any case not a primitive feature but a later development. A solution to this problem was found in the Pauline pneumatology with its concept of the life-giving Spirit to which the effects of baptism could now be attributed. With this development a double role was now envisaged for the Spirit in christian initiation, in baptism and in confirmation. While the unified solemn rite prevailed, a sharp distinction could be avoided here by viewing the whole process as a complex unity and by following in commentary a salvation history approach which allowed appeal to different concepts of the Spirit at appropriate moments. With this approach the life-giving concept came to characterise the role of the Spirit in baptism, the prophetic that in confirmation. It was inevitable in these circumstances that an explicit assertion of two gifts of the Spirit in christian initiation would eventually emerge. This assertion comes with St. Augustine. When the separation of the two sacraments becomes established practice, and their unity as together constituting the one process of initiation consequently becomes difficult to envisage, this assertion now provides a way of maintaining the separate elements in some form of coherent focus. The Spirit is given in baptism as the source of the new life there conferred. Later, the Spirit is given again in confirmation as a prophetic strengthening or endowment of the life received in baptism.

The statement of the Carolingians, and especially that of Rabanus Maurus, accurately summarises and completes this evolving tradition. The theological enterprise of the later Middle Ages will be very dependent on the textual sources available to it, *auctoritates*. On the question of confirmation, the Carolingian statement will keep it in vital contact with the great patristic tradition.

CENTRAL MEDIEVAL PERIOD

The theology of confirmation in the scholastic theologians of the twelfth and thirteenth centuries has to be approached and understood in the light of the textual sources on the question available to them. Apart from the Bible, these consisted mainly of some patristic texts, especially the works of St. Augustine; the sermon of Faustus available in the ninth century compilation known as the Psuedo-Isidorian Decretals and attributed there to a (non-existent) Pope Melchiades; the comments of the Carolingians, particularly Alcuin and Rabanus; and various odd texts available in collections such as the *Decretum* of Gratian. However limited in scope this body of texts may seem, it does echo the basic themes of the western tradition on the gift of the Spirit in christian initiation. These sources, therefore, maintained the medieval scholastics in continuity with that tradition and enabled them to attempt their own assessment of it.

The basic theological text-book of the central and later Middle Ages was the *Four Books of Sentences* of Peter Lombard, written around the year 1155. This was the text studied and lectured on in the theology schools and discussed by theological authors in their commentaries. Lombard's basic statement on the meaning of confirmation is clear and direct.

> The effect of the sacrament is a giving of the Holy Spirit for strengthening who in baptism was given for remission (of sins) (*Sentences* IV, dist. 7).

This summary statement has by now a familiar ring. Augustine's assertion of two gifts of the Spirit is again highlighted, while Faustus' term *robur* continues to characterise the confirmational gift. This statement forms the basis of the discussion of confirmation in later scholastic theology. It will be a question simply of fleshing out its implications. The Spirit is given in baptism as the source of its effects and as the indwelling presence of God. The Spirit is given again in confirmation for strengthening. The basic question is how this strengthening, which defines the meaning of confirmation, is to be understood.

On this issue St. Thomas Aquinas can again be taken as the best representative and the most original contributor of the medieval galaxy. His mature theology of confirmation appears in the *Summa Theologiae* III, q. 72. Aquinas here seeks to define the strengthening which the gift of the Spirit in confirmation involves. He first describes this effect as conferring what he calls "a kind of adult age of the spiritual life". (*Sum. Th.*, q. 72, art. 1).[16] This phrase, much commented on in modern writing on confirmation, though not always accurately, requires careful interpretation, if Aquinas' meaning is not to be misrepresented. He indicates clearly that he is not thinking of a strict analogy between physical development and the christian life. He is not referring to any particular age, to any form of personality development or to any formal act of commitment which might be thought to mark entry into mature life. He is thinking rather of the social aspect of the Christian's life, of the quality and power it possesses when lived publicly before the world as a witness of Christ, a preaching of the gospel, a sermon in action. The Spirit informs this witness with his own special strength or force. He sums up his concept of the gift of the Spirit in confirmation as follows: "The confirmed person receives power to profess the faith of Christ publicly in words, as it were, officially" (*Sum. Th.* q. 72, art. 5). The

[16]For a study of St. Thomas' theology of confirmation, see J. Latreille, "L'Effet de la Confirmation chez St. Thomas D'Aquin, *Revue Thomiste*, 57 (1957), 29-52; 58 (1958), 214-243.

public profession of the faith in the power of the Spirit, this is the special strength which confirmation confers. This is what the analogy of adult age signifies in this context.

It is clear that Aquinas' understanding of confirmation is derived primarily from the statement of Rabanus Maurus and the tradition which it represents. With this understanding, Aquinas places himself solidly in the tradition which sees confirmation as characterised by a gift of the prophetic Spirit. He does not describe this effect as bluntly as Alcuin and Rabanus as ordained to preaching. By this time canonical concepts have developed and insist that preaching is an official hierarchical act of the Church requiring a formal *missio canonica*. Aquinas has, therefore, to find an alternative expression to the *ad praedicandum* of the Carolingians and he opts for the language of public profession of faith. The scope of the concept as he envisages it may seem a somewhat narrow one: the primary example he adduces is a situation of persecution where the Christian must be prepared to bear witness to the faith before its enemies. Despite the change of terminology, this is the same concept as that of the Carolingians. Aquinas conceives the effect of confirmation as a special force given by the Spirit for the public profession of the faith. For him, also, therefore, the gift of the prophetic Spirit is what characterises the sacrament of confirmation.

Aquinas' theology of confirmation and its relation to baptism is but a further expression of the established western tradition on this issue. There are two gifts of the Spirit in christian initiation: in baptism as the source of divine life, in confirmation as the gift of prophetic force. Confirmation, as Aquinas insists, completes the initiation begun at baptism and together with baptism constitutes full christian initiation, the making of the full Christian and member of the Church. Here Aquinas, though his terminology and approach may differ somewhat, is at one with the Carolingians and St. Augustine. The Council of Florence, therefore, in seeking a summary statement of this tradition, did not err in adopting this theology of Aquinas.

EVALUATION

The meaning of dogma, it has been said, is its history. This certainly, I think, applies to the theology of confirmation. The understanding of the sacrament which became established in the West is a product of its history, of the intertwined history of its liturgy and its theology. Once the development of this tradition is seen as a whole, it appears as fully logical and consistent. It is realized quite early that a role has to be attributed to the Spirit in baptism, despite the absence of reference to such a role in the original practice, apart from the Pauline theology. But once this role is granted, then it becomes a question of defining and distinguishing the double role now attributed to the Spirit in the sacraments of initiation. The required distinction is ready to hand in the concepts of the Spirit as life-giving and prophetic and theological effort proceeds to develop its understanding on the basis of this distinction. The Pauline pneumatology, with its integration of the christological and peneumatological references, thus comes to characterise the baptismal role of the Spirit, and the Lucan the confirmational. In this perspective, St. Augustine's assertion of two gifts of the Spirit in initiation was logical. Later writers, faced with the sharp separation of the sacraments in actual practice, gladly appealed to this notion as a way of maintaining both the relation and the distinction between baptism and confirmation. The statement of this theology which eventually emerges as authoritative is St. Thomas Aquinas' formulation of the Carolingian understanding.

In the last analysis, this theology has to be assessed on the basis of its effort to understand the role of the Spirit in christian initiation. Here a basic problem emerges. The New Testament does not speak of two gifts of the Spirit, but of one, however many aspects it may recognise within that one gift. The Johannine and Lucan accounts of the giving of the Spirit do not refer to different events; they are simply different presentations of the one event. The New Testament, therefore, does not support a parceling out of the role of the

Spirit in initiation in the sharp terms of two distinct gifts. The theology, whose development we have been following, attempted with this concept to forge a unity for the separate moments and references of the initiation rite. It can scarcely be said to have succeeded in this enterprise and this theological task still awaits achievement.

This criticism, however, should not blind one to the achievements of this theology. It has argued convincingly that the Spirit is involved in the whole process of christian initiation, that to think of christian initiation without the activity of the Spirit of God is not possible. It has also emphasised that confirmation is a sacrament of initiation, that it constitutes with baptism the full process of initiation. Confirmation, therefore, is not concerned with an optional state of life within the Church, as marriage or ordination, but with the making of the Christian and member of the Church. The significance of these fundamental assertions for an understanding of christian initiation today will occupy us in the next chapter.

Chapter Eight

CHRISTIAN INITIATION TODAY

Renewal

Sacraments are a celebration of the christian community's life in Christ.[1] A sacrament exists to be performed, to be celebrated. This is its purpose and meaning. Sacraments, therefore, are not simply objects of academic study. Such study is necessary and important, but it too must serve the ultimate purpose of sacrament, its celebration. Concern with the sacraments of initiation today exemplifies this observation.

The Church's practice and understanding of christian initiation has come down through the centuries shaped by the interacting history of practice and theological thought. As this movement entered the twentieth century, the impression is inevitable that the development had proceeded in a narrowing direction and had ultimately resulted in a rigidity and ossification of thought and practice. The rite of christian initiation, from being a unified, solemn and impressive

---

[1] The subjects of this rite are decribed in the Introduction as follows: "Children or infants are those who have not yet reached the age of discernment and therefore cannot have or profess personal faith."

celebration of the community initiating new members, had disintegrated into two distinct rites separated by a considerable interval of time. Baptism was administered in infancy, with the old adult rite adapted for this purpose. The ceremony had lost its public communal character and had become a private, individualistic practice administered by the priest in Latin.

A significant loss in this development was the disappearance of the catechumenal catechesis. This catechesis had preserved and constantly repeated in the Church the biblical understanding and presentation of christian initiation and involved an annual reminding of the Church itself of the meaning of its practice. With the disappearance of this instruction in this presentation of baptism, the whole sense of the new creation theme in all its aspects was left largely unexpressed. To be fully appreciated, the rite itself required this instruction. The power of the rite itself to speak was now also seriously hampered by its being celebrated in what was, in effect, a dead language. Only the doctrine of baptism remained as a commentary on the rite. But since this was a doctrine concerning special questions, it did not purport to be, nor could it serve as, a presentation of the sacrament as required by the rite. The sacrament of baptism required a breath of life to revitalise its actual celebration.

The separation of confirmation from baptism had given this sacrament an independent existence over against baptism and had thus made explicit the question of its meaning. We have already spoken of the different aspects of this complex question as it presents itself today. We have also traced the history of the sacrament and its theological understanding. We saw how the theological tradition came to speak of two gifts of the Spirit in christian initiation, in baptism and confirmation, and saw the latter as conferring a "strengthening" on the baptized. The purpose of this strengthening was for the public profession of faith, but the weak pneumatology of the Western Church was not able to clarify this concept sufficiently or adequately retrieve the biblical and patristic concept of the prophetic Spirit which was its source. Further, the separate existence of the sacrament made it difficult to see it as a sacrament of initiation or to appreciate how it formed a unity with baptism, the unity of christian initiation.

It was inevitable that concern for the meaning and practice of initiation would draw attention to these and other related issues. The early decades of this century saw the appearance of many scholarly studies devoted to the history and meaning of christian worship and its rites. These studies helped to situate the current state of christian liturgy in its historical context, revealed the factors which had been at work in this development and the deficiencies which had been accumulated along the road. This scholarly study initiated a new concern for the practical aspects and values of liturgy. The "liturgical movement" was born. This concern for liturgy was based on the conviction that the public prayer and worship of the Church was the centre of its life, the pole around which that life revolved. The demand was for a living liturgy, a way of performing communal worship which would be a disclosive experience of God's presence through Christ in the Spirit.

The eucharist, as the Church's central sacrament and act of worship, naturally received the major attention in these studies. But the other sacraments were not neglected and baptism in particular was the subject of many scholarly works which had a big impact on the understanding of the sacrament. Confirmation has not received anything like this attention and much ground work still remains to be done in this area. As was said in the previous chapter, this has hampered modern commentators on the rite who seek to answer questions of pastoral concern about the sacrament.

Following on the interest and enlightenment created by these studies, the sacraments of initiation became the subject of a new pastoral interest. It was felt that the new insights and understanding had pastoral implications which, if fully worked out, could lead the way to a true renewal of sacramental celebration. The announcement of the Second Vatican Council provided the advocates of liturgical renewal in the Catholic Church with their opportunity. Much of the scholarly study on liturgy had already been accomplished by the time of the Council and many of the scholars were at hand to explain their work and present their ideas. The eventual result was the Constitution on the Liturgy, *Sacrosanctum Concilium*, one of the finest documents of the Vatican II corpus and the one which history may well judge of most lasting significance. The document outlined the fundamental concepts of christian liturgy and laid down basic guidelines for a thorough renewal of the liturgy to be undertaken after the Council. Over the following years this programme was taken in hand and eventually issued in new rites for all the sacraments. Among these were new rites for the sacraments of initiation.

The Revised Rites

In all, three new or revised rites were issued for christian initiation. These were: the Rite of Baptism of Children (1969), the Rite of Confirmation (1971), the Rite of Initiation of Adults (1972). Previously, it must be recalled, only two rites existed, a rite of baptism common to all, infants and adults, and the confirmation rite. The first major change, therefore, was the issuing of two rites of baptism, one for infants and children and another for adults. Moreover, the adult rite is a full rite of initiation, it comprises the celebration of baptism and confirmation in the one ceremony as in the old solemn rite. The unified rite of christian initiation involving baptism and confirmation is here restored. Further, the catechumenate also is restored as the formal process of preparing adult candidates for initiation and a basic structure, sensibly flexible and adaptable, regarding its form is laid down. The new rite for confirmation administered on its own has, in fact, little new about it. It is basically the old Roman rite of confirmation issued again. The occasions on which priests may administer the sacrament are extended, but this was a situation which had been developing for a number of years. The formula pronounced by the minister at the chrismation of the forehead, which only became fixed in the Middle Ages and was rather unexpressive, was altered to:

Be sealed with the Gift of the Holy Spirit.

a formula similar to that used in the Greek Orthodox Church, a sensible ecumenical gesture. One regrettable feature, however, is the declaration that the chrismation and its formula constitute the essential action and words of the sacrament.

> The Sacrament of Confirmation is conferred through the anointing with chrism on the forehead, which is done by the laying on of the hand, and through the words: *Accipe Signaculum Doni Spiritus Sancti. (Rite of Confirmation: Apostolic Constitution,* 1971).

Though this statement was intended as a practical decision, it unwittingly affects the unity of the rite and downgrades to some extent the importance of the opening prayer and gesture, the epiclesis of the seven-fold Spirit. In the old Roman rite this prayer said with outstretched hands over all the candidates was quite central and the individual imposition of hand and chrismation which followed it represented the effective application of this prayer for each candidate. The whole rite thus formed a clear unity. Opting for the chrismation as the *essential* action interferes with this unity, however unintentionally, and one would hope that sometime this decision might be revised.[2]

These new rites represent a major renewal of its initiation liturgy by the Catholic Church. They merit detailed attention and analysis, but it will not be possible to pursue such detail here. For this the reader is directed to the texts of the Rites themselves and their Introductions and to the many fine commentaries which have appeared.[3] Attention here

[2]For comment on this question, see: A. Nocent, "Vicissitude du Rituel de la Confirmation," *Nouvelle Revue Theologique*, 94 (1972) 705-720; L. Ligier, "La Priere et Le Imposition des Mains. Autour du Nouveau Rituel de la Confirmation," *Gregorianum*, 53 (1972) 407-486.

[3]As well as the text and rubrics of the rites themselves, the Introductions also merit careful attention. See *Introductions on the Revised Roman Rites* (London, Collins, 1979). For an interesting commentary on the revised rites, see A. Kavanagh, *The Shape of Baptism: The Rite of Christian Initiation. (N.Y., Pueblo Publishing Co., 1978).*

will concentrate rather on more basic issues. When I said, assessing the historical development of the initiation rites, that this development consisted of a haphazard adaptation to changing historical circumstances. It was a development which lacked a guiding concept. This cannot be said of these new rites. While no revolution is here attempted, these rites have clearly been well thought out and planned and they embody and implement a concept of christian initiation appropriate to the situation of our times. The most useful task which can be undertaken here is to attempt to identify this concept and its more important manifestations.

For disclosing this concept the most significant of the new rites is undoubtedly the Rite of Initiation of Adults. This rite is not simply a practical measure required by the decision to issue a special rite of baptism for infants and children, and thus cater to adult converts. Its significance goes much deeper than that. The restoration here of the unified ceremony of christian initiation, manifesting once more the unity of baptism and confirmation as sacraments of initiation, is quite epoch-making and reverses the disintegration of the rite which history had imposed. But more basic is the acknowledgement, implied at least by the Rite, that christian initiation in its comprehensive sense is concerned with producing a mature member of the Church, one who is able to personally appropriate the gift of faith and commit himself or herself to the life of faith. Such a person is what the process of initiation seeks to achieve. The sacramental initiation rites are not the whole of this process, though they are a very significant part of it. Recognition of this aim of initiation is simply common sense and in fact has always been the policy of the Church. The initiation rite and process of the early Church, as we have seen, was mainly concerned with adults and the rite was devised with adults in mind. Adult initiation here was the norm, not only in the statistical sense but also in terms of principle. The care and thoroughness of the catechumenal preparation, the emphases of the sacramental rite, the care shown the new Christians in the early period after their initiation, all this shows that the Church's interest lay in testing and forming mature members of its community of faith. This was the principle and the norm. The new Rite of Initiation of Adults makes us aware again of this principle and norm.

Recognition of this principle is in no way an acknowledgement of the baptist practice, that only a believer's baptism is valid. The Church has always, implicitly at least, acknowledged this principle, while at the same time practicing and encouraging the baptism of infants and children. There is really no conflict between the principle that ultimate membership of the Church is mature membership and the practice of infant baptism. In fact, it is this principle which allows infant baptism to be seen in its true context. The Church has always opposed indiscriminate baptism and the occurrence of such has always been in defiance of canon law. It has always insisted that baptism must have a faith context which will support the candidate in his or her faith and enable them to grow and develop in the faith to mature membership. In the case of infant baptism, it has looked to the parents and sponsors, to the faith of the local community in which the infant is baptised and in which it will grow up, to its own system of religious education and formation, to supply this context. This means that in the case of infant baptism the Church does not see the *process* of initiation as completed with the administration of baptism. In fact, it sees this process in this case as simply beginning. Juridically, the baptized infant is a member of the Church. But a long process of formation in the faith has only now begun and will continue until this infant has reached mature status and is able to personally appropriate and make its own the promises made in its name at baptism.[4] In effect, what the catechumenate sought to achieve *before* baptism in the case of the adult convert is undertaken by an even longer process of religious formation and education in the case of the infant *after* baptism. But in both situations the aim is the same: mature membership of the Church. The Rite of Initiation of Adults reminds us again of this principle and norm.

---

[4]*See especially Rite of Baptism of Children: Introduction 2-3.*

In doing so, it enables us to see infant baptism in its true context and enables us also, as we shall see, to give a coherent meaning to the separation of baptism and confirmation in this context.

Another striking emphasis in these new rites is their public communal character. The shape and text of the rites leave no doubt that the community is centrally involved in their celebration. We have already remarked on many occasions how the ceremony of baptism had come to lose its public character and had become a private rite performed by the priest. Yet, it has always been a basic principle of sacramental theology that it is the Church which celebrates the sacraments; the role of the minister is not a private role; he acts in the name of the community and as its focus. The Second Vatican Council defined the Church as the People of God. Concretely, this is the local worshipping community. The sacramental principle and the ecclesiological, stating but different aspects of the one reality, show that it is the worshipping community which acts in the celebration of sacraments, with the minister performing an essential role, not apart from, but within that community and in its name.

The most dramatic implementation of this principle occurs in the Rite of Baptism of Children. The old rite of baptism, as we have seen, had been devised for adult candidates and had addressed them as active participants. When infants became almost exclusively the candidates for baptism, this rite was adapted, rather haphazardly and not very happily, to their condition. The new rite, fully acknowledging that these candidates "cannot have or profess personal faith," addresses not the candidates but the community receiving those candidates into membership, and especially the parents and godparents as the community representatives here most intimately concerned. It is the community itself which here answers for the infants, professes faith in their name, goes guarantor for that faith and commits itself to bringing up these children in that faith. The congregation present is actively participant and a main actor in this ceremony. It celebrates the sacrament.

This same emphasis on public communal character is also

evident, *mutatis mutandis*, in the other rites. For example, the Rite of Initiation of Adults states:

> The initiation of catechumens takes place step by step in the midst of the community of the faithful. Together with the catechumens, the faithful reflect upon the value of the paschal mystery, renew their own conversion, and by their example lead the catechumens to obey the Holy Spirit more generously. (*Introduction*, 4).

One further instance which might be mentioned is the oft stated preference that these rites be performed at Easter, Pentecost, or Sundays and during Mass, in other words, on the liturgically significant occasions and when a representative body of the community are gathered together.

In restoring the unified rite of christian initiation, in acknowledging that the ultimate aim of initiation is the mature, committed member of the Church and in insisting on the public communal character of these celebrations, these new Rites present a fundamental, coherent concept of christian initiation. It is a concept which retrieves and implements once more the form and character of initiation in its classic period. Such a concept has many implications and applications, many of which run counter to the general practice imposed by the later historical development of the rites. It will take time for these various implications to be identified, for conflicts with prevailing practice to be smoothed out, for the retrieved concept to be implemented in a coherent, practical system. The Rite of Initiation of Adults, in particular, is a new phenomenon and its actual use and relevance will obviously vary greatly from place to place. But from the point of view of a concept of christian initiation, this Rite is of universal relevance and significance and merits close study and attention. It will take time for the Church to absorb the concept inherent in these new rites and to adjust its inherited practice to the demands of this concept.

Meanwhile, there remains one particular question which deserves more extended comment. What light do the new rites throw on the question of confirmation?

The Question of Confirmation Again

At first sight it would appear that little if any new light is thrown on the problem of confirmation by the new rites. As was said earlier, there is little new in the Rite of Confirmation itself. The comments on the meaning of the sacrament in the Introduction are also quite traditional and break no new theological ground. Above all, the issuing of a separate Rite of Confirmation leaves untouched the old questions and problems which arise precisely from this separation. Despite this, however, I think the Rites do throw a significant new light on this old question and point the way to a coherent view of the relation of baptism and confirmation when these sacraments are conferred separately .

Let us recall that the problem, as it presents itself today, arose from the separation of confirmation from baptism in the rite of initiation and the need then felt to give a distinct meaning to this sacrament over against baptism. The required distinction was found in the two biblical concepts of the Spirit, life-giving and prophetic. The Spirit was seen as active in baptism, as the source of the new life there conferred. The gift of the Spirit in confirmation complemented and completed this endowment with a gift of prophetic force for christian witness and the public profession of faith. Theology, though not significantly the rites themselves, thus came to speak of two gifts of the Spirit in christian initiation: a gift of the life-giving Spirit in baptism and a gift of the prophetic Spirit in confirmation.

The problem with this theology arises first from its source, which is an assumption, namely, that the separate celebration of these sacraments must mean that they have totally distinct, independent effects, however complementary these effects may be in other respects. The two sacraments were defined over against one another, in terms of their contradistinction rather than in terms of their intimate relation. Starting from this assumption, the theology which rests on it cannot but be rather artificial, whatever other values it may contain. The suggestion of two gifts of the Spirit in initiation is such an artificial construction. There is no basis for this suggestion in the New Testament. We have seen how the idea of two gifts of the Spirit separates too sharply baptism and confirmation and does not do justice to the unity which they constitute as sacraments of initiation.

In re-thinking this question with the aid of the concept presented by the new rites, it is well first to remind ourselves of this unity of christian initiation.

Confirmation is a sacrament of initiation; it is not a later sacramental event in the life of the fully initiated Christian. The question of the relation of baptism and confirmation depends, therefore, on the way christian initiation is envisaged. Here the concept presented by the new rites can make a significant contribution. The separation of these sacraments first occurred, ironically enough, as an attempt to maintain the unity of initiation by insisting on the presence of the bishop to complete the ceremony as in the old solemn rite. But in the context of almost exclusively infant baptism, the separation developed into a definite system involving a considerable interval of years. The separation of the sacraments belongs basically to this context of infant baptism and later confirmation and it is from within this context that it has to be approached and assessed.

The determining factor here must be the recognition that the fully initiated member of the Church is the mature member. This is the *terminus ad quem* in the light of which the whole process of initiation has to be assessed. Until this point is reached some aspect of initiation has been left incomplete and remains to be accomplished. The rites of initiation have to be significantly related to this on-going process. Where the adult convert is concerned, there is no problem here: the full initiation rite comes as the climax of the catechumenal preparation and concludes it. The problem is very different, however, in the context of infant baptism. Here the process is a lengthy one and consists of growth in the community, a process of formation and education in the life and faith of the community adapted to the different stages of the child's development. The process is complete when this basic education has been given and the young person is deemed capable of personally appropriating the formation in faith he or she has received.

The practice of the Church, East and West, has varied greatly over the centuries in the way it has related the rites of initiation to this process of the young person's growth in faith. The East has opted for a complete initiation rite, baptism and confirmation, at infancy; the West has separated baptism and confirmation by a varying interval of years. However accidental the origins of this western practice may have been, it has endured over the centuries. It must, therefore, have some merit, as otherwise it would be difficult to account for its survival. In any case, it is the long-standing, prevailing practice and is recognised as such in the new rites. The question is how the unity of baptism and confirmation is preserved in this practice.

A first observation on this question must be a warning. The word "unity" should not be conceived too simply and, especially, it should not be confused with the unity we associate with a moment of time. A story, a novel, has a unity, even though it may take hours or hundreds of pages to relate, may cover a very wide span of time and involve a lengthy sequence of episodes and a kaleidoscope of images and symbols. Similarly, a person's life is a unity, even though it may span many decades and involve a bewildering variety of experience and adventure. Indeed, it may be and has been argued that the whole of history is a unity, a process with an alpha and an omega. Unity, therefore, is determined by the nature of the object in question; it is not a construct imposed on the object by the thinking subject. The unity of baptism and confirmation should not be approached too simplistically and in an *a priori* fashion. The unified rite of initiation is entitled to be regarded as the standard and norm. But it presupposes a particular set of circumstances: the adult convert, the catechumenate, the full rite of initiation. The context of infant baptism presents a different set of circumstances and this difference, with all its implications for the unity of the initiation sacraments, has to be respected.

In contrast to the situation of the adult convert, whose formation and education in faith begins with the catechumenate and precedes baptism, in the case of the baptised infant this process begins *after* the baptism and is conducted by and within the community which has accepted this responsibility at the baptism. In other words, the catechetical process which now gradually gets under way corresponds, *mutatis mutandis*, to the catechumenate which precedes baptism in the case of the adult. Viewing the catechetical process in this light, where should confirmation figure in relation to it? The significant place for confirmation in this context would certainly seem to be at the conclusion of this process, as the climax of this basic formation in faith. Without in any way suggesting that confirmation is the sacrament of natural or physical adult age, the sacrament would here have something of the character of an adult initiation rite and yet would retain its relation with baptism as completing the rite of initiation begun at baptism. The two sacraments would here frame the initiation process of the young person marking its beginning and its end. Seen in this way, and bearing in mind the previous comments on the concept of unity, baptism and confirmation, though separated in time, would still be seen to constitute the one, full rite of christian initiation. Moreover, these rites would now also have a significant relationship with the catechetical formation of the candidates and enable this process to take on more explicitly than is now the case an initiation character.

When baptism and confirmation are related in this way in terms of their unity, a theological issue arises and requires attention. Does the gift of the Spirit take place at baptism or is the Spirit only given later at confirmation? In addressing this question, it must first be noted that terms such as "gift," "given," can convey a definiteness, a reference to a precise moment of time which is not quite appropriate to the Spirit whose activity is not subject to such control. The limitations of such terms have to be borne in mind. The gift of the Spirit refers really to entering the Spirit-filled community and thereby sharing in the Spirit which fills and animates the community. When full membership of the community is understood as mature membership, the entry of the infant, child, young person, into such membership is necessarily a process of growth. In this context the gift of the Spirit is also a process and not simply a once-for-all moment of time. To clarify further this observation, it may be helpful to recall some points already made concerning the sacraments of initiation.

Christian initiation expresses the basic qualities of the community into which the person is being received. In its origin the rites of initiation expressed the two experientially distinct but intimately connected events which founded the Church and maintained it in existence, the event of Christ and the event of the Spirit. In its origin, then, christian initiation possessed two basic references: christological (baptism) and pneumatological (the rite of the Spirit or confirmation). Further theological reflection revealed more and more the intimate connection of these references. The Spirit was the Spirit of Christ, the Spirit of life in Christ. The Spirit is therefore already implied in the christological reference of baptism. yet, the Church, following the salvation history pattern of the rites, continued to practice the post-baptismal rite formally referring to and celebrating the gift of the Spirit. This rite, whenever administered, is a rite of initiation which with baptism confers membership of the Church.

All sacramental theology is by implication ecclesiology and the operating concept of the Church determines the character of the sacramental theology. The concept of Church which has been most influential here has been the institutional concept. But this is a rather static concept and it needs to be complemented by other models, for example and by way of shorthand, the concept of Church as event. There is a true sense in which the Church was not merely founded once-for-all so many centuries ago, but is founded continually every new day. Christian initiation gives membership of the Church. When the Church is seen simply as institution, membership will be regarded in a rather juridical sense, a question of status and rights determining meaning and limits of participation. Such a static concept of membership has to be complemented by a more dynamic one which conceives membership in terms of event, process, growth. Such membership will be seen as leading the Christian not into a merely passive, docile status within the institution, but into the full freedom of mature human and christian personality.

An ecclesiology which sees the Church simply as institution will have difficulty giving proper place to the concept of the Holy Spirit. In the Creed we profess belief "in the Holy Spirit in the holy Catholic Church," that is, as the animating presence in the Church, the source of its continual life and mission. This presence of the Spirit can only adequately be expressed by a more dynamic concept of Church. Similarly, the terminology of "gift" as used of the Spirit must likewise not be confined to a purely static juridical sense. The child growing up in the community is growing into the community and therefore growing in the Spirit which fills the community. There is a developing and dynamic giving of the Spirit throughout this process until it is completed. In the context of infant baptism, baptism expresses the beginning of this gift and growth in the Spirit and confirmation its completion. The pneumatological reference thus pervades, implicitly or explicitly, the whole rite of initiation. But the theme of the Spirit is particularly appropriate to the conclusion of the process which heralds entry into mature and responsible membership of the Church. Here the dynamic concept of the Church as the Temple of the Holy Spirit has special relevance.

If in the context of infant baptism the relation of baptism and confirmation is viewed in this way, it would seem logical that confirmation should be conferred at a somewhat later age than is at present customary. A flexibility on this question is allowed by the new rite. If mature membership of the Church is a determining factor, some period in mid-teenage would seem an appropriate time. Some implications of such a system merit a mention here in concluding these comments on the question of confirmation.

This slightly later age for confirmation would enable the ecclesial character of the sacrament to stand out more clearly. Confirmation would appear as the completion of the rite and process of christian initiation giving full entry into and membership of the Church. The important theme of the Spirit in the Church would receive a significant expression in this context. Central to the celebration of the sacrament would be the concept of the Church as the Spirit-filled community of Christ, the terrain where the soil and climate should foster the growth of the fruits of the Spirit. Confirmation here would be both a significant reminder to the community of its own identity and the promise it is offering the candidates and an invitation to the candidates to appreciate this concept of the Church. It is important, of course, that the candidates' subsequent experience of the Church should not contradict this meaning and promise. But an important occasion would here present itself where the Church would realize herself as the Spirit-filled body of Christ.

A further feature of this context for confirmation concerns catechetical formation and education. This formation could now more formally appear as the initiation process which it is and be given its true initiation character. Catechetical formation would constitute a significant part of the process which reaches completion with the reception of confirmation. Since mature, responsible membership of the Church is the ultimate purpose of this process, it seems obvious that such formation should not be purely academic or school and classroom centered, but situated rather in the life of the living Church community. The programme should involve the young person in the life and mission of the Church at parish and diocesan levels. The Church is not simply a formula to be learnt, but a community life to be shared in and experienced. The young person's initiation and growth into the community should involve active participation in its life. Only so can true appreciation of what Church means develop. The necessary doctrinal instruction in the faith could only benefit from this context.

In devising such a programme, the carefully planned structure of the adult catechumenate could perhaps supply some inspiration. It contains features which, suitably adapted, could usefully figure in a catechetical programme conceived along these lines. Examples which come to mind are: distinguishing stages in the progress of the process, the involvement of the community in the preparation of the candidates, the liturgical expression given to the catechumenal status. This similarity between the later confirmation and the adult rite is worthy of attention.

The Question of First Communion

If one views the relation of infant baptism and later confirmation in this way, a special question arises concerning the place of first communion. Should the present practice be continued, where children make their first communion some years before confirmation or, as some writers today maintain, should first communion be postponed until the occasion of confirmation itself, thereby restoring the classic sequence of baptism — confirmation — eucharist?

It is certainly true, as we have seen, that in the classic concept and practice of christian initiation full participation in the eucharist was the climax of the whole process and rite. As I said at the beginning of this work, participation in the eucharist is the achievement of christian initiation. The classic norm for the order of the initiation sacraments is undoubtedly baptism, confirmation, eucharist. Those who advocate a return to this sequence in the context of infant baptism and later confirmation can therefore base their argument on solid theological and historical grounds. Indeed, if confirmation were conferred in the period between seven and ten, the argument cannot, in fact, be gainsaid. But if confirmation is postponed to a later age, and especially if it is most appropriately conferred in mid-teenage, as I have been advocating, then I think other factors enter the picture and alter the case. In this situation I do not think first communion should be postponed for so long and the argument for earlier communion now, in my opinion, takes precedence. Contrary to what might at first sight appear, I do not think this position contradicts the classic norm. To justify this assertion, however, a brief discussion of the question will be necessary.

It is a significant fact in the history of christian initiation that, once baptism and confirmation became separated in practice, the placing of first communion also became subject to considerable variation. Sometimes it occurred before confirmation, sometimes after. Our current practice developed only in the latter part of the last century and was reinforced by the decree of Pope Pius X that children should receive first communion about the age of seven, that is, on arrival at the age of discretion. While at first sight it would seem that this practice contradicts the classic norm on the sequence of the initiation sacraments, it is necessary to bear in mind that the norm presupposes the situation of the adult convert and the whole process of the adult catechumenate. The context of infant baptism and later confirmation presents a very different set of circumstances. A norm which is derived from one particular situation should not be too simplistically applied to another. As I have been emphasizing, christian faith in its full sense is a mature faith, the faith of the mature person. The classic norm of christian initiation is derived from a realistic working out and application of this principle in the situation of adult converts. It is this situation which establishes this norm. But the situation of infant baptism and later confirmation has special features peculiar to itself which have to be respected and given their due weight. If one were to apply directly the adult norm to this situation, there is a distinct danger that much of the realism which characterises it in its own situation may be lost. The norm itself, in its own name and from its own nature, may require modification when a different context is envisaged.

That the initiation of infants and children possessed peculiarities of its own is clear even in the classic period from the adaptations of the adult rite which were required, for example, the use of sponsors to answer for the child. Today one must also take into account the very great differences in social conditions between the ancient world and our own. The upbringing and development of a child today is very different indeed to what it was in ancient times. The growth of the child and young person into modern society is a much longer and more complex process than in former times. The development and formation in faith of the young person is part of this overall process. It, too, therefore, differs greatly from the formation which would have taken place and been sufficient in the past. There is a great contrast between the simplicity and even pace of life in former ages and the complexity and rapid pace which characterise our world. This contrast in social conditions between past and present, which we so easily take for granted, should alert us against too easily applying norms derived from the past to conditions in the present, especially where the young are concerned.

If, in the context of infant baptism, confirmation is viewed as I have presented it, that is, as constituting the completion of initiation and entry into mature membership of Christ and his Church, then it seems very difficult to maintain that the young person developing in faith and growing into the community of faith should for so long be deprived of full participation in the eucharist, the very centre of the community's life. Experience of the eucharist and of union with Christ in communion is a very important and significant experience in the life of a young person and in his or her growth in faith. A process of initiation towards mature faith during these significant years of life is surely considerably strengthened by this experience. If this is so, then surely all contrary arguments must cede to this consideration.

If confirmation, in the context in which we are speaking, meant the first conferring of the Spirit on the baptized, that prior to this their christian life was not life in the Spirit, then indeed the argument that full participation in the eucharist should follow confirmation would be absolutely cogent. But this is not the case. We have seen that according to the Church's developed reflection, the pneumatological reference of initiation pervades the whole rite, even if the formal moment of its assertion and expression is confirmation. The baptism of an infant brings the child within the Spirit-filled community of Christ's disciples. Henceforth, the child is in

Christ and in the Spirit of Christ. Growth in and into this community, which the process of initiation begun in baptism involves, develops and deepens relationship with the community to the point where the process is complete and the young person is deemed a fully mature member of the Church. I have argued that the formal celebration of the gift of the Spirit in confirmation has a special significance and appropriateness at this point. But since the young person is through baptism already within the community and therefore lives in the Spirit, it simply cannot be maintained that communion should be postponed on the ground that it has not received the Spirit. I quoted earlier the statement from the General Introduction to the Rite of Baptism of Children: "Baptism is the sacrament by which men and women are incorporated into the Church, built into a house where God lives, in the Spirit, into a holy nation and a royal priesthood." Since the baptized young person is within the worshipping community and growing in this community, participation in the eucharist should be part of its life and of its development towards full membership. In these circumstances the process of initiation to mature membership requires this. Certainly, confirmation, which here marks the arrival at mature status, should and normally will take place within the celebration of the eucharist and this eucharist will draw its own solemnity from this context and possess its own sense of climax. But there is no theologically cogent reason for maintaining that full participation in the eucharist and reception of communion should be postponed until this occasion.

The view which I am expressing here, in the context of infant baptism and confirmation at a mature age, and in support of the sequence baptism-eucharist-confirmation in this context, does not contradict the norm for the older of these sacraments which holds in the case of adult converts, the norm that is established in the rite of initiation in the classic period. The infant baptism – later confirmation context has features of its own which have to be taken into account and one should not impose the adult norm too simply on this context without considering the import of these features. The situation of the adult is different to that of the child growing in faith and in the community of faith. The view of infant baptism and later confirmation which I am presenting is, I believe, a realistic and theologically sound understanding of what the process and rite of christian initiation involve in this context. While there are differences between the two contexts, these are not as substantial as they appear at first sight. It is the same *concept* of christian initiation which is in question in both situations. It is the actual working out and application of this concept to the different circumstances which give rise to the differences. The differences themselves are not fundamental.

Theology Again

The interest in christian initiation which has developed in the course of this century has been largely pastoral and liturgical. Discussion has tended to concentrate on how to revitalise the celebration of these sacraments, how to ensure effective celebration. This concern eventually led to the revision of the rites which we now possess. This programme has involved an impressive array of scholarship. The many and different aspects of christian initiation in their historical and theological dimensions have been the subject of much study. The theology of initiation involves many of the basic themes of christian faith, for example, Christ, Spirit, Church, faith, christian life. The new studies and approaches in these various areas have thus helped also in the renewal of the theology of initiation. The pastoral, liturgical concentration has not, therefore, meant any lessening of interest in the theology of initiation, but has rather stimulated the theological enterprise. The general orientations of this modern theology of christian initiation have, I hope, already been sufficiently presented in this work. But by way of conclusion a brief word might be said on some topics which have been mentioned already in the course of our study.

The question of the relation between faith and baptism, the role of faith in the sacrament, has remained a live one in our time. What is the respective contribution of faith and baptism in achieving the effects of the sacrament? It would be a serious mistake in approaching this question to see these roles as in opposition to one another, to suppose that the effects have to be attributed to either one or the other or partly to one, partly to the other. Rightly understood, the sacramental principle does not admit of such a simple dichotomy of objective and subjective elements. In the catholic tradition sacraments are presented as sacraments of faith, and baptism in particular is presented as *sacramentum fidei*. Faith, in other words, is an essential element of sacrament, part of its very definition. One cannot, then, oppose faith and baptism and discuss their relation in terms of such opposition.

The meaning of the term "faith" in this context is obviously important. Faith here cannot be restricted to the doctrinal sense of belief, the assent of the intellect to truths revealed. It must be understood rather in its more comprehensive biblical sense where the personal dimensions of trust and commitment are also included. In this sense faith is a direction of one's being, an entrusting of oneself to God through Christ in the Spirit. Such faith has undoubtedly an intellectual, doctrinal content. One must have some understanding of God to whom one commits oneself and what that commitment involves. But the faith which sacrament involves includes all these deeply personal dimensions. It is living faith.

Sacraments are sacraments of faith in a double sense. They are so called, first, because the celebration of the sacrament is an expression of the faith of the Church. The Church is here expressing its very being, its life in Christ, and this is an expression of its faith. Likewise, the subjects' reception of the sacrament is an expression of their faith. It is their faith which has led them to the sacrament and their participation in the rite is an expression of this faith. The ritual of baptism provides a good example of how a sacrament is such an expression, both on the part of the celebrating community and the receiving subjects. Throughout the rite the Church is proclaiming in faith the Gospel of salvation, and the subjects assent to this proclamation. All the actions, gestures, prayers, formulas which constitute the rite form part of this expression. In baptism this faith context appears especially in the candidates' assent to the Creed, the Church's official summary of its faith. It will be recalled that originally this reception of the Creed was part of the act of baptism itself. The coincidence of sacrament and faith stands out most clearly here. Faith and baptism are not distinct entities within the action of initiation. On the part of the celebrating Church and the receiving subjects, baptism is an expression of faith. In this expression Christ is present receiving new disciples.

It follows from this that the faith in question here is not the purely private faith of an individual. Faith here means first and foremost the faith of the christian community, the faith of the Church. The individual shares in this faith by membership of the community and professing its faith. Christian faith is never a purely private matter. It is the public faith of the christian community. Since baptism is the formal moment of entry into the Church, it is also the moment of entry into the Church's faith. Prior to this moment, the faith of the subject, however full and whole-hearted it may have been in all other respects, was not yet christian faith in the true, formal sense. It was still a private stance. By entering the community of faith through baptism, the candidate receives the faith of the community and makes this public faith his or her own. Henceforward, their faith will be the faith of the Church.

This point is brought out clearly in the rite of baptism itself. The opening of the old rite, and still an optional opening in the new, asks the candidate: "What do you ask of the Church of God?" To this question the candidate replies simply: "Faith." The candidate comes to baptism asking for faith, the faith of the Church. Baptism in giving entry into the Church gives the candidate this faith, this life. We saw earlier that this is the teaching of the New Testament. Oscar Cullman in his study of the sacrament in the New Testament sums it up succinctly: "Baptism is the starting point of faith."

Discussion of the relation between faith and baptism naturally brings to mind the question of infant baptism. We have already spoken of the basic issue involved here but a word might usefully be said on some aspects of this question as it presents itself today. Historically, direct evidence of the practice can be traced back to the second century A.D. There is no direct, explicit reference to infant baptism in the New Testament, but this does not constitute an argument from silence. The Jewish background to christian baptism, the arguable implication of a number of New Testament passages and the unquestioned practice of the Church so soon after the New Testament period all warrant the conclusion that infants and children were baptised in the Church from the beginning. Eventually, as we know, apart from missionary situations, infants became the almost exclusive subjects of baptism. This remained the unquestioned practice until the Reformation, when a wing of Protestantism, the Anabaptists, following a particular interpretation and application of the Reformation principle of justification by faith alone, maintained that only those sufficiently mature to make a personal act of faith could receive baptism. The main Protestant Churches, Lutheran and Calvinist, rejected this position and stood by the old practice. Today the main representative of the Anabaptist position is the Baptist Church.

The question of infant baptism became a live issue again in Protestant theology in this century following a lecture delivered by Karl Barth in 1943 and published some years later. In this paper Barth rejected the practice in the name of the Reformation principle. His stance initiated a controversy which called forth numerous defences of the traditional practice by Protestant theologians. The Catholic Church remained largely unaffected by this Protestant controversy. It still insists not merely on the validity but on the importance of the baptism of infants. Nevertheless, while there is no theological questioning of the practice, misgivings are sometimes expressed today on pastoral grounds. The basis for these misgivings would seem to be that the faith context which infant baptism requires cannot nowadays be automatically presupposed. When society and culture were still strongly christian, little problem arose here. The child grew up in this christian environment and was formed by it. Today, however, it is sometimes felt the pluralist character of society no longer provides this context and the christian upbringing of infants cannot be so easily presupposed. This clearly is a weighty consideration, but it would seem to be a question of pastoral approach rather than a matter of theological principle. Obviously, much depends on the particular context, especially of the home and the parents, but also on how the christian community itself responds to the challenge of its environment. Ultimately, it would seem it is a question of the vitality of the community and the effectiveness of its system of catechetical formation. The theological principles, at least, are clear. Infant baptism is a valid practice, but the sacrament here only begins a long process of christian initiation which should eventually culminate in mature committed membership of the Church. The challenge of our times is to devise a pastoral system which can achieve that goal.

CONCLUSION

The subject of christian initiation, in all its breadth and depth, embraces a wide range of topics and concerns. We have not been able in the course of this study to cover all this ground or discuss all the issues.[1] Like so many other movements in history, the meaning and implications of christian initiation are illuminated especially by a consideration of its origins. A study of the practice in the early Church shows that its foundation lies in the ministry of Jesus, in his meeting with people and his call to them to become his disciples, and in the gift of the Spirit after his resurrection. These events brought into existence the Spirit-filled community of Jesus' disciples. Here Christ still lives, still issues his call to discipleship and offers the gift of his Spirit. To accept this offer is to become a member of the community and live with its life. It is to be given an identity, the true and ultimate identity which comes from relationship with

---

[1]One particular aspect of christian initiation with which I have not been able to deal within the confines of this study is the significant ecumenical discussion of recent years. But interested readers now have available to them the important Lima Report of the World Council of Churches, *Baptism, Eucharist and Ministry* (Faith and Order Paper No. 111, WCC, Geneva, 1982), and the theological comentary edited by Max Thurian, *Ecumenical Perspectives on Baptism, Eucharist and Ministry* (Geneva, WCC, 1982).

God through his Son in the power of the Spirit. The giving of this identity is a grace, a gift. It is the gift of community, of participation in the christian fellowship which is the Body of Christ. In the midst of all the ambiguities and negativities of history, this is the identity, the definition, the salvation which humanity longs for and seeks. It is the gift of access to God, of rest in God.

> Through him (Christ) we have access to the Father in the one Spirit. (*Ephesians* 2, 18).

The Church is bound by the command of its Lord to offer this grace to the world throughout history, to make disciples of all nations. In its practice and process of christian initiation it continually seeks to fulfill this command. This is a basic aspect of its mission. In its sacraments of initiation it offers the gift of true life, discipleship of Jesus Christ, the Way, the Truth and the Life.

Recommended Reading

E.C. Whitaker, *Documents of the Baptismal Liturgy*. (London: SPCK, 1970[2]).

E. Yarnold, *The Awe-Inspiring Rites of Initiation: Baptismal Homilies of the Fourth Century*. (London: St. Paul's Publications, 1971).

A. Hamman, ed., *Baptism: Ancient Liturgies and Patristic Texts*. (Staten Island, Alba House, 1967).

A.G. Martimort, ed., *L'Eglise en Priere*. (Paris: Desclee, 1965[3]). Part of this work has been translated into English as *The Church at Prayer* (Irish University Press, 1968).

M. Dujarier, *A History of the Catechumenate*. (N.Y.: Sadlier, 1979).

L.L. Mitchell, *Baptismal Anointing*. (London, SPCK, 1965).

J.D.C. Fisher, *Christian Initiation: Baptism in the Medieval West*. (London: SPCK, 1965).

J. Danielou, *The Bible and the Liturgy*. (Notre Dame Press, 1965).

P. Pourrat, *Theology of the Sacraments*. (London and St. Louis: Herder, 1930).

B. Neunheuser, *Baptism and Confirmation* (London and Freiburg: Herder — Burns and Oates, 1964).

L. Brockett, *The Theology of Baptism*. (Cork: Mercier Press, 1971).

B. Leeming, *Principles of Sacramental Theology*. (London: Longmans, Green, 1956).

J.P. Schanz, *The Sacraments of Life and Worship*. (Milwaukee, Bruce, 1966).

A. Hamman, *Bapteme et Confirmation* (Paris, Desclee, 1969).

K. Rahner, *The Church and the Sacraments*. (Edinburgh-London: Nelson, 1963).

_____, *The Rites of the Catholic Church.* (N.Y.: Pueblo Publishing Co., 1976).

_____, *Introductions on the Revised Roman Rites.* (London, Collins, 1979).

C. Flanagan, ed., *Making the Most of the Ritual Readings.* (Dublin, Dominican Publications, 1978).

Mark Searle, *Christening: The Making of Christians,* (Essex, Mayhew, 1977).

A. Kavanagh, *The Shape of Baptism: The Rite of Christian Initiation.* (N.Y.: Pueblo Publishing Co., 1978).

_____, *Made, Not Born. New Perspectives on Christian Initiation and the Catechumenate.* (Murphy Centre for Liturgical Research, Notre Dame Press, 1976).

L. Ligier, *La Confirmation: Sens et Conjoncture Oecumenique Hier et Aujourd'hui.* (Paris: Beauchesne, 1973).

G. Wainwright, *Christian Initiation.* (Richmond, John Knox Press, 1969).

_____, *Baptism, Eucharist and Ministry.* (Geneva: WCC, Faith and Order Paper No. 111, 1982).

Max Thurian, ed., *Ecumenical Perspectives on Baptism, Eucharist and Ministry.* (Geneva, WCC, 1982).